Introduction

I F YOU MENTION THE WORD *Catholicism* to many people, the first things that come to mind might be the smells and bells of the ancient liturgy, the pope addressing the faithful outside St. Peter's Basilica, public controversies surrounding euthanasia and abortion, aid agencies working with the poor in the developing nations, or maybe more sinister images, like those in Dan Brown's *Da Vinci Code* or the Spanish Inquisition. Something less readily associated with Catholicism in the popular mind is the firm imperative addressed to all members of the Church to *evangelize*. Indeed, evangelization is more commonly associated with other religious groups, those who knock on doors or give out leaflets on street corners, or who tread lonely paths with a sandwich board predicting imminent doom and an urgent need to repent. It might therefore come as a surprise to some that the unanimous witness of the three nodal points of Catholic theology—Scripture, Tradition, and Magisterium—claims that all members of the Body of Christ are under an imperative to carry Christ's message to all the people of this world.[1]

Within the Church, this imperative is much more readily recognized among the faithful than it was some decades ago, having been articulated by numerous magisterial documents, and reiterated by successive popes following on particularly from Paul VI's *Evangelii Nuntiandi* of 1975.[2] That said, when one looks more closely at the question of what evangelization should look like in the contemporary world, or what shape the work of this New Evangelization should take, the answers one receives can be very different. Some, for example, present evangelization as something that seeks to find shared values or points of contact with aspects of contemporary cultures, while others strike a markedly *counter*-cultural note, presenting evangelization as a basic challenge to dominant cultural norms for the sake of the Catholic alternative. There are good grounds to suggest, therefore, that although the imperative to evangelize is generally recognized within the Church as incumbent on all the faithful, the actual *form* (or the "how") of fulfilling this imperative is much more open to question.[3]

This ambiguity stems from a fundamental tension that is one of the most basic issues facing Christian theology. This tension is the issue of accommodation. When speaking of accommodating the witness or proclamation of the faith to others, two opposing stimuli come into play. Believers are called to bear witness or to proclaim their faith, to let people know the message of salvation and invite them to share the fellowship of Christ in the Church. On the one hand, of course, this calling requires that the witness given or the message proclaimed has meaning for those who see and hear it, and thus offers something significant to their lives. The witness or message, therefore, needs to be accommodated to the circumstances in question, in the sense that the Latin root verb *accommodare* means "to fit one thing to another." The first stimulus thus encourages the "fitting" of the witness or the message to terms others can understand and acknowledge, to finding points of contact or resonances between the faith and their worldviews, to show thereby how sacramental life in Christ has bearing on who they are.

On the other hand, it is equally clear that the witness or message is not to be restrained or diluted by this process of being fitted to the expectations of others. Christ says, "I am...the truth" (John 14:6), and what is coming to faith if not the surrender of one's presuppositions and expectations in obedient acknowledgment of that truth? Or, as put by *Dei Filius*, faith is "the full *submission* of [the] will and intellect to the God who reveals."[4] A second stimulus now comes into view, in which the witness or the proclamation must be preserved in its genuine authenticity—it must remain a true expression of the faith itself. This stimulus still provokes an accommodation, but here we are dealing with an accommodation in the sense of a "residing" or an "inhabiting," meaning the truth of the faith can "inhabit" the lives of others in its full authenticity, and not be detrimentally fitted to terms improper to it. If we take these two stimuli together, the evangelizer has the challenging task of judging how to "fit" the content of

MARY, STAR OF EVANGELIZATION

Dear John,

You're an inspiration!

MARY,
Star of Evangelization

TILLING THE SOIL AND SOWING THE SEED

JACOB PHILLIPS

Paulist Press
New York / Mahwah, NJ

Library of Congress Cataloging-in-Publication Data
Names: Phillips, Jacob, author.
Title: Mary, star of evangelization : tilling the soil and sowing the seed / Jacob Phillips.
Description: New York : Paulist Press, 2018. | Includes bibliographical references and index.
Identifiers: LCCN 2017058941 (print) | LCCN 2018026243 (ebook) | ISBN 9781587687044 (ebook) | ISBN 9780809153374 (pbk. : alk. paper)
Subjects: LCSH: Evangelistic work—Catholic Church. | Mary, Blessed Virgin, Saint.
Classification: LCC BX2347.4 (ebook) | LCC BX2347.4 .P485 2018 (print) | DDC 266/.2—dc23
LC record available at https://lccn.loc.gov/2017058941

ISBN 978-0-8091-5337-4 (paperback)
ISBN 978-1-58768-704-4 (e-book)

Published by Paulist Press
997 Macarthur Boulevard
Mahwah, New Jersey 07430

www.paulistpress.com

Printed and bound in the
United States of America

For my mother

Contents

Preface

THIS BOOK BEGAN LIFE through my being commissioned to write a course booklet for a postgraduate module ("Evangelising Culture") at the Maryvale Institute, Birmingham, in the United Kingdom. My gratitude is first and foremost due, therefore, to Dr. Stephen Yates, program director for Maryvale's MA in Catholic Applied Theology, for conceiving of this project and overseeing its preliminary stages. I am also deeply indebted to my friend and colleague, Dr. Stephen Bullivant, director of the Benedict XVI Centre for Religion and Society at St. Mary's University, Twickenham, United Kingdom. Stephen not only encouraged me to work the original course booklet into a full publication, but introduced me to Paulist Press as a possible outlet. I am very grateful to Paul McMahon at Paulist for his encouragement and patience as the manuscript was underway. I would also like to mention two students from the Evangelising Culture module: Caroline Sanderson and Fr. Thom Amungwa, for their attentiveness and the fruitful responses they offered to the material in this book. While writing, I was teaching at Allen Hall Seminary in London, so I'm grateful to the vice rector, Fr. Michael O'Boy, and rector Fr. Roger Taylor for enabling my ample use of the Allen Hall library, and for welcoming me to their community Mass and meals. I would also mention seminarian Jon Stogdon, with whom I had some helpful discussions about this project early on. Most of all I owe thanks to my wife, Soheila, and our son Eli, from whom I learn far more than I could read in any book.

the faith to the means by which others can make sense of it, while at the same time preserving or maintaining what is irremovably necessary to it, so it can "inhabit" or perdure genuinely *as itself* when communicated and is not lost in the expectations and presuppositions of the addressee.

In speaking of worldviews, or sets of expectations or presuppositions, we are pointing toward the patterns of collective self-understanding or "webs of significance"[5] that have long been grouped under the concept of culture. The word *culture*—although ubiquitous in contemporary discourse—requires some definition for the purposes of our discussion, a task undertaken in the first chapter. For now, it suffices to say that, in the ambiguity underlying the "how" of evangelization, there are theological concerns involved in the relationship between faith and culture. This relationship is the concern of this book, which sets out to discuss the parameters involved in relating faith and culture, with a view to providing answers to the question of "how" exactly evangelization ought to proceed. While outlining some paradigmatic examples of different strategies for orienting the work of evangelization, we will study the theological coordinates at play in the judgements that those who are involved in evangelizing must make when "fitting" the faith to the worldviews of others while ensuring it is transmitted in its authentic truth.

Faith, of course, arises from a living *call*, an invitation to live differently that makes its home in the hearts of its hearers, calling them to something genuinely new (Rom 6:4; Rev 21:5). However, faith itself is a human *response*, and for people to respond, there must be a meeting point with the means by which people understand life and the world. In presenting different strategies for seeking to bring others to faith, and setting out their theological bases in relation to culture, this book seeks to cast new light on these discussions by approaching them through the figure of the Virgin Mary. In other words, we will examine a Marian pattern for considering the relation of faith and culture in evangelization, showing the Blessed Virgin as the point where the differing strategies on offer in Catholic theology converge. In this way, the multifarious impulses at work in theological understandings of evangelization will have an exemplary Marian focal point and, as we will see, have potential to be informed by Marian piety.

Mary is highly appropriate to this endeavor as a point of convergence for different theological coordinates, because it is in Mary that the divine call and its perfect response coalesce. This calls to mind Joseph Ratzinger's discussion of the relation between Mary and traditions of divine Wisdom (*Chokmah*), or *Sophia*, in the Old Testament, as part of his aim to show how the figure of Mary in the New Testament "is woven entirely of Old Testament threads."[6] As is well known, in the Old Testament *Sophia* literature, Wisdom seems, at times, to be a primordial personification of God's creative energy, a divine "Word" or "imprint" existing with God before all ages (cf. Wis 9:9).[7] For this reason, the New Testament draws deeply on this tradition in exploring the person of Jesus Christ (cf. 1 Cor 1:24). Ratzinger points out that Wisdom was approached through an exclusively christological lens by many theologians in the mid-twentieth century, and taken thereby as referring only to Christ, the *Logos*, "the divine call of creation and election" proclaimed by "the Word who establishes wisdom." At the same time, however, wisdom is also a human quality (cf. Sir 1:10–12), seen in the virtue of prudence, a quality that speaks of good judgement and an ever-deepening lived responsiveness to the will of God. Considering this point, Ratzinger argues that an exclusively christological approach to *Sophia* is somewhat restricted, for the responsiveness of faith—the taking root of wisdom in humanity—requires "a pure answer" that enables God's creative Word to "find its irrevocable dwelling place" among human beings. Ratzinger argues that this answer is itself an integral aspect of the Old Testament Wisdom-*Sophia* tradition, an aspect that "resists total integration into Christology"; it is the response to the call, the response of one who "receives wisdom and brings it to fruition."[8] Insofar as the figure of Mary is woven from these strands of the tradition, then, we can consider her a meeting point of call and response, a place where God's creative Word not only dwells, but also grows and is formed in loving responsiveness to God's will. This dynamic mirrors the challenge facing the work of evangelization, which involves imparting the authentic call to faith without dissolution, while at the same time seeking to enable or cultivate a genuine response in the addressee.

Mariology is not the first thing that comes to mind in discussing evangelization, but these dynamics involved in the Wisdom-*Sophia* tradition suggest it is a highly promising avenue to explore the challenges of interrelating faith and culture in evangelization. Some pointers in this direction have been provided for us through the prevalence of a recent title of Mary: "the Star of the New Evangelization." This title has a strong magisterial pedigree, being rooted originally in Paul VI's *Evangelii Nuntiandi* (§82), reiterated frequently by John Paul II and Benedict XVI,[9] and discussed in some length as the climax to Pope Francis's *Evangelii Gaudium* (§§285–88). Notwithstanding this pedigree, however, the detail of what the title means is not always immediately forthcoming. Of course, it alludes to the star that led the Magi to Christ (Matt 2:1–12), but why is Mary presented as the great beacon of evangelization when there is no account of her explicitly evangelizing in the Scriptures? Pope Francis gives us some clues for answering this question in *Evangelii Gaudium*. He writes that "through her many titles, often linked to her shrines, Mary shares the history of each people which has received the Gospel and she becomes part of their historic identity" (§286). Traditions of Marian devotion thus signify the deep-taking root in a host culture of the faith of the gospel. He goes on to state that Mary is also deeply connected with both the "pursuit of justice," as "she who praised God for 'bringing down the mighty from their thrones' and 'sending the rich away empty' (Luke 1:52–53)," and also the more contemplative disposition that ponders and ruminates the "mystery of God in our world" (§288). For Pope Francis, then, there is a "Marian 'style' to the Church's work of evangelization," through an "interplay" of "contemplation and concern for others," thus making her a supreme "model of evangelization" (§288).

In this passage from *Evangelii Gaudium*, there is a contrast with Ratzinger's concentration on Mary as a reminder of the responsiveness of faith, which he associates with a certain passivity and docility. In this connection, he mentions St. Louis de Montfort's quoting of the prophet Haggai—"You do much but nothing comes of it" (Hag 1:6)—to describe the problems with considering the work of the Church purely in terms of activity, or what he calls "expenditure of energy."[10] We might want to ask ourselves, here, if this quote applies to some evangelization initiatives of recent years. Either way, to lessen this contrast between Pope Francis's "concern for others" and Ratzinger's view of Mary as a cipher for passivity and "waiting," it is worthwhile pointing to the link between docility as responsiveness to God's will, and responsiveness as taking responsibility for the welfare of others, a link clearly perceptible in theological understandings of love as a mutually enriching and intrinsically inseparable love of God *and* neighbor.[11] The issues at stake in evangelization return here, for Ratzinger calls the Church "the living seed of God that must be allowed to grow and ripen," and this growth and ripening is something that requires the docility involved in our becoming "waiting, inwardly recollected people who in the depth of prayer, longing, and faith give the Word room to grow."[12] In this sense, Mary emerges not only as the locus of a response, but equally as the locus of preserving or guarding the conditions enabling the "living seed" of Christ's call to take root. Indeed, the connection of Mary with purity soon comes to mind, here, as something broader than physical chastity, for, in maintaining the genuine authenticity of Christ's call, an evangelizer is called to maintain the purity of that call. Moreover, Mary is held by tradition to be immaculately conceived, and this is the supreme theological expression of what is termed prevenient grace, which in this context is a "preventing" of dissolution and adulteration, or a "preserving" of the purity of the call. In this book, then, Mary is regarded as a point where both accommodating or "fitting" the call to the situation of the addressee, and maintaining its authenticity so it can genuinely dwell within the addressee's heart, come together. In what follows, we will explore this "Marian style": first, studying closely the tension at work in evangelization and outlining its Marian application, then second, delineating how the inquiry will take shape in the subsequent chapters.

THE CENTRAL AXIS OF EVANGELIZATION IN A MARIAN KEY

The Central Axis

With the root issue beneath the ambiguity in evangelization being centered on accommodation, it is no surprise that the two stimuli on either side of this ambiguity are aptly articulated by the foundational document of contemporary Catholic evangelization, *Evangelii Nuntiandi*. Interestingly, however, this document does not present this tension so much as a problem, but as two constitutive conditions that define evangelization. Paul VI presents the meeting point of these two stimuli as the moment at which evangelization takes place: when the witness or message makes sense to others while remaining authentically itself—when Christ's proclamation "I am the truth" is disclosed as the truth striking someone to the heart while making sense according to his or her understanding of life. Paul VI speaks of the meeting of these two stimuli as "the central axis of evangelization," saying that "fidelity both to a message whose servants we are and to the people to whom we must transmit it living and intact is *the central axis of evangelization*" (*Evangelii Nuntiandi* 4, au. emphasis). The word *axis* means "pivot"—the line around which a globe turns—suggesting the meeting of these two stimuli is the fundamental pivot on which evangelization turns. To analyze this "central axis," let us look first at Paul VI's own description of it, and show the precedents for each side of it in Scripture, Tradition, and magisterial teaching, before showing how each of these sides promises to have light shed on it through the figure of Mary.

Paul VI states that when evangelizing, "it is absolutely necessary for us to take into account a heritage of faith that the Church has the duty of preserving in its untouchable purity" (*Evangelii Nuntiandi* 3). Approaching this preservation of purity through Scripture, it is clear that at the very origins of Christianity, Jesus was hardly one to shirk the difficulties of challenging the worldview of his hearers. Of course, this was the faith of the Hebrew Scriptures as practiced by his contemporaries, particularly the scribes and Pharisees. There are a great many examples of this, such as Jesus openly proclaiming in the synagogue, leading some to exclaim, "Is not this Joseph's son?" before becoming enraged and seeking to kill him (Luke 4:16–29), or the Pharisees picking up stones to throw at him after he states, "Before Abraham was, I am" (John 8:58–59). This resistance stems from the fact that what Jesus proclaims does not fit comfortably with the expectations of the society of his day. First, no one expected divinely authenticated teaching to come from the son of a nondescript local carpenter. Second, it was unthinkable to the Pharisees that Jesus himself could be of divine origin, have been with God before all ages, even before the founding father, Abraham, himself. In the first instance, Jesus claims to have a messianic authority that far exceeds what people expected of him, and in the second, an authority that far exceeds even what was expected of the Messiah.

Examples such as these indicate that Jesus's proclamation not only met with serious resistance, but that he did not shy away from conflict, and continued to proclaim the truth of his message in what Paul IV calls its "untouchable purity." In short, Jesus does not seem to have been willing to "fit" his proclamation to the expectations of his audiences. This tendency, of course, continues in the Catholic tradition through martyrdom, a word that comes from the Greek μαρτυς (*martus*), meaning "witness." The cult of the martyrs begins in the New Testament, with St. Stephen (Acts 7), but became widespread during the first Christian centuries. A well-known, early example is St. Justin Martyr, who was denounced in AD 163 and put on trial, where he refused to sacrifice to the pagan gods of the Roman Empire.[13] Moreover, magisterial teachings of recent decades provide us with many apt illustrations of "preserving" the "untouchable purity" of the message of faith. The conciliar document *Gaudium et Spes*, for example, while claiming that the Church is interested in one thing only—"to carry forward the work of Christ" in bearing "witness to the truth" (§3), admits that people are "often diverted from doing good and spurred toward and by [their] social circumstances" (§25). For this reason, we read, "Christ's Church" still "cannot help echoing the Apostle's warning: 'Be not conformed to this world' (Rom. 12:2)" (§37). We thus see a preservation of "the heritage of faith" in its "untouchable purity," or what *Gaudium et Spes* describes as a "living fidelity" to this heritage of tradition (§56).

But, as noted previously, in *Evangelii Nuntiandi*, this commendation of fidelity to the authentic teachings of the faith is only one side of what might be termed a double-pronged fidelity in evangelization. Paul IV not only writes that "it is absolutely necessary for us to take into account a heritage of faith that the Church has the duty of preserving in its untouchable purity," but also speaks "of presenting it to the people of our time, in a way that is as understandable and persuasive as possible" (*Evangelii Nuntiandi* 3). When we look at the handing on of the message of Christ across the centuries, there are numerous examples of a certain "fitting" to the cultural context in question. A scriptural *locus classicus* of this "fitting" is seen with Paul in Athens (Acts 17), using the image of the Athenian "altar to an unknown God" as a point of contact or resonance that would make sense to his hearers, thus making the message as "understandable and persuasive as possible" by saying, "What therefore you worship as unknown, this I proclaim to you" (Acts 17:23). In the development of the Catholic tradition, we need only look at how the faith has taken shape in such different forms throughout the centuries, to see this same pattern at work. One can easily compare the dizzying array of diverse cultures at work in, say, the ornately illustrated Lindisfarne Gospels, a Gothic masterpiece like Chartres Cathedral, the neoclassical majesty of St. Peter's Basilica, Leonardo da Vinci's *Virgin of the Rocks*, a technicolor Romero Cross, the Divine Mercy image of St. Faustina's Poland, and George Rouault's expressionist painting of 1936, *The Crucifixion*.

The concern for "fittingness" is also firmly established in magisterial teaching, such as *Gaudium et Spes*, again, which states that "in language intelligible to each generation, [the Church] can respond to the perennial questions which [people] ask about this present life and the life to come" (§4). The document then states that in faith, the people of God "labors to decipher authentic signs of God's presence and purpose in the happenings, needs and desires in which this People has a part along with other men of our age" (§11). The Council fathers thus claim that certain aspects of the modern world provide helpfully constructive values to which evangelization can be fitted, enabling the message to be made as "understandable and persuasive as possible," including the prevalence of the "exact" sciences (natural sciences), a new "mass-culture from which are born new ways of thinking, acting and making use of leisure," and the "increase of commerce between the various nations and human groups" (§54). These characteristics are subsequently affirmed as largely "positive values," insofar as the "exact" sciences can exhibit a "fidelity toward truth in scientific inquiries," or how the "increase of commerce between the various nations and human groups" can exhibit "a sense of international solidarity" (§57). In this passage, the Council fathers find points of contact between the message of Christ and his Church and the expectations of the prevailing culture, a resonance between the *values* of nonreligious human activity on the one hand, and the revelation of God in Christ on the other.

Mary and the Central Axis

Consequently, following the "central axis" of *Evangelii Nuntiandi*, we can approach evangelization as something that happens when the content of the faith in its "untouchable purity" is expressed in a manner that is "as understandable and persuasive as possible" according to the demands of a specific cultural setting. As mentioned earlier, defining exactly what culture means will require some attention later, but to give a preliminary indication, let us bear in mind that the original Latin word for culture is *cultura*, an agricultural term meaning "a cultivating," in the sense of cultivating plants and crops. Culture thus refers to the development or fostering of something, so just as a farmer cultivates the land to grow fruit and grain, human endeavors are *cultural* insofar as they develop or nurture something and bring it to fruition; insofar as they are themselves the fruit of this nurturing. The root verb of *cultura*, *colere*, brings a further dimension of meaning, referring to "tending, guarding, tilling." We can think of a farmer as one who guards the land, by overseeing it, protecting it from predators, overturning it, weeding it, and watering it to bring fruits to bear. Similarly, we can extend this to wider human endeavors to oversee and protect those activities that might bring the best fruits of human nature to birth.

So, culture in its original meaning is concerned with the *human*—human "webs of significance," systems of "meaning-making" or organs of value. In this sense, there are grounds to suggest that culture deals with fostering our humanity, for culture surely affirms human uniqueness and dignity in the created world. This is perhaps why Paul Lehman states that culture refers to the process required "to make and to keep human beings human."[14] Indeed, here we continue to see the relevance of the Latin word *cultura*—insofar as the cultivation of human nature is compared to tilling the "soil," to make it "cultured" or productive, and the Latin word for soil is *humus*, which has led one commentator to speak of culture involving "a transition from *humus* to *homo*," a movement from raw nature to genuine humanity.[15] That is, as the farmer takes the raw material of soil and ensures it bears fruit, culture takes the raw material of human nature and nurtures the fruit of values therefrom.

Paul VI's central axis points to a "planting of the seed" or "taking root" of Christ that requires that the message is made "as understandable and persuasive as possible," and it is a point of fact that the ways in which human beings understand life and the world are cultural. Culture thus presents itself as that which structures the response to God's call, that which demarcates the contours of the yes to the invitation of faith. There-fore, in making the message as "understandable and persuasive as pos-sible," we need to give attention to the soil on which the seed of Christ's teaching is sown and not merely the seed itself. Here, we find another indication of the worth of approaching this inquiry through the figure of Mary, for the Virgin Mary is the one from whom the human stock of Christ is drawn, and it is in the human soil (or *humus*) of Mary's womb that Christ is made human (*et homo factus est*), and at the hands of Mary's parental stewardship that he is formed in his humanity at Nazareth.

Indeed, it is highly instructive, here, that Mary has, from some of the earliest times of Christianity, been approached symbolically through images like the *good* or *immaculate soil*. Terms like *unstained, pure,* or *immaculate* link Mary with soil or earth, and are found as early as the Acts of Andrew, thought to have been written around AD 150–200. The nomenclature stems from the forming of Adam from the earth of the Garden of Eden, when the world is unstained by sin. This connects with the patristic development of understandings of Mary as the New Eve, drawing particularly on the Fourth Gospel (e.g., John 19:26–27), and seen explicitly in Justin Martyr, Irenaeus, and Tertullian.[16] It is a relatively straightforward step from here to consider Mary as the unstained, immaculate, or pure earth in which the Spirit breathed life in conceiving Christ at the annunciation. But this symbolism of Mary as immaculate earth (*terra immaculata*) was not merely a devotional or theological type, but is extended by the fathers into something in which human beings can participate, in a sense imitating the *terra immaculata* through fostering the conditions that can bring Christ forth in their lives. For this reason, Origen, Gregory of Nazianzus, and Gregory of Nyssa all speak of the souls of the faithful being conformed to Mary, with Gregory of Nyssa speaking of the soul as "living earth of a man's heart," to extend what Origen describes by saying "just as an infant is formed in the womb, so it seems to me the Word of God is [formed] in the heart of a soul."[17] This idea of the soul as a womb, and the faithful thus "birthing" Christ in their lives, reaches an apogee in Ambrose, who draws on the account of Christ addressing Magdalen as directly as "Mary" in the resurrection garden (a place symbolically reminiscent of the Garden of Eden), and argues that Christ's use of the name Mary, here, indicates that "when the soul begins to turn to Christ, she is addressed as 'Mary'…for she has become a soul who in a spiritual sense gives birth to Christ."[18]

Regarding Mary as the *terra immaculata*, and the subjective appropriation of this symbol to the human soul in writers like Ambrose, we can understand why Ratzinger approaches the parable of the sower through Mary, as the "good soil" on which (or in whom) the seed of the Word bears plentiful fruit. Again, we see here an approach to Mary as the locus of a response, for he writes that the "mystery of Mary means precisely that God's Word did not remain alone; rather, it assimilated the other—the soil—into itself, [and] became man in the 'soil' of his Mother."[19] As we have seen, the cultural is the intrinsically human—the means by which we are "made and kept" human, so Mary promises to offer an exemplar of good human soil, appropriately cultivated ground on which or in which Christ can take root in the hearts of human beings. In this sense, we can now see how one side of Paul VI's central axis—making the message "as understandable and persuasive as possible"—can be approached though the figure of Mary, for the point of contact whereby the message can be understood and found compelling is the soil of human culture, and so an evangelizer needs to be sensitive interpreting his or her cultural context, tilling and guarding the good within it, and finding the places—points of contact—where the message might take root.

At the same time, however, let us remember here also Pope Francis's words that Mary is called the Star of the New Evangelization though the interplay of both active and receptive dimensions to her person, of "contemplation and concern for others," and the connection of Mary with preserving the seed in its authenticity (*Evangelii Gaudium* 288). This would suggest that the figure of Mary is not only an archetype of the ground on which the message is sown, but something more dynamic or potent. That is, Mary is not only the locus of a response, but is bound up with the very call itself, in whom both call and response coalesce as with the Old Testament Wisdom-*Sophia* tradition. The more active side to Mary is alluded to in the rococo Marian devotionalism of St. Louis de Montfort, who himself speaks superfluously of Mary as "a virginal and immaculate earth" who makes Christ "fertile and fruit-bearing," but also draws on the Wisdom-*Sophia* tradition in apportioning a command made to the divine Wisdom to Mary herself: "'strike the roots of all your virtues in my elect' (cf. Ecclesiasticus 24:13)."[20] Mary is thus connected not only with the soil on which the seed is sown, but also with the sowing of the seed itself of Christ's word by preserving its authenticity. Therefore, we can discern the other side of exploring the interrelation of faith and culture through the figure of Mary, as she promises to offer resources for the other side to Paul VI's central axis. That is, she both offers a key for assessing the cultural grounds by which an evangelizer can make the "message as understandable and persuasive as possible," precisely *while* "preserving" its "untouchable purity." Mary emerges here as a locus whereby Christ's proclamation is disclosed authentically as itself and makes its home in someone's heart, while being fitted at the very center of that person's worldview. This duality thus offers us an exemplary Marian focal point through which to explore the interrelation of faith and culture in the work of evangelization in the following chapters.

TILLING THE SOIL AND SOWING THE SEED

The subsequent chapters will explore faith and culture through the figure of Mary, the Star of Evangelization, and present the work of evangelization thereby as both *tilling the soil* and *sowing the seed*. To provide more detail about how this will proceed, note first that the active-dynamic duality in question is rooted in traditions of Marian devotion, such as the Litany of Loreto, some of which provides a framework for the later chapters.[21] Mary has numerous titles in this litany, which seem to present her as both a dynamic, active figure, like *virgo praedicanda* (Virgin to be preached/proclaimed) or *Turris Davidica* (Tower of David), and a passive, receptive figure, like *Vas spiritual* (spiritual vessel) and *Vas honorabile* (Seat of wisdom). This ancient Marian devotion thus generally corresponds with the two-sidedness to Mary outlined earlier, but it also promises to be fruitful as a prime example of the tendency of Marian devotions to emerge from grassroots levels, from the practices of the simple faithful. This feature of Marian devotionalism connects with a concern for evangelization, for it provides an optimum illustration of successful evangelization itself. That is, devotions like the Litany of Loreto are the fruit of the teaching of the gospel that has taken root deeply in people's hearts, the fruit of truly evangelized cultures.

We have seen that this is recognized by Pope Francis in his insight that the frequently localized nature of Marian devotion is connected to her title as the Star of the New Evangelization (see *Evangelii Gaudium* 286). There is a precedent for this approach in John Paul II's address *Ecclesia in America*, which focuses on the popular piety so commonly associated with South American Catholicism, and, like *Evangelii Gaudium*, mentions Our Lady of Guadalupe as particularly emblematic of a distinctively Latino Marian devotion: "an impressive example of a perfectly inculturated evangelization" (*Ecclesia in America* 11).[22] We will examine in more detail the term *inculturation* in chapters 3 and 4, but for now, let us concentrate more closely on this pointer to popular piety in Marian devotion as emblematic of a fruitful evangelization.

Earlier in *Evangelii Gaudium*, Pope Francis writes that "expressions of popular piety have much to teach us," and "for those who are capable of reading them," they can function as a "*locus theologicus* which demands our attention" (*Evangelii Gaudium* 126). He goes on to suggest that focusing on popular piety can, in a sense, reconfigure our relationship to the content of the faith, in that he claims that popular devotionalism "discovers and expresses [the content of the faith] more by way of symbols than by discursive reasoning." This is based on his claim that the practices of popular piety show that "in the act of faith greater accent is placed on *credere in Deum* [belief in God] than on *credere Deum* [belief *about* God]" (*Evangelii Gaudium* 124).[23] This distinction, coming from Thomas Aquinas,[24] demarcates believing *in* God (a living, relational, and dynamic faith), from believing *that* God exists (holding to a proposition about God). This is a straightforward distinction between believing "in," or "knowing" on a personal level, as opposed to holding to certain convictions "about," as a propositional, conceptual knowing. This is the difference between saying, "I am rationally convinced the world must have a first cause," and saying, "Oh my Jesus, have mercy on me a sinner!" For this reason, for Francis, the expression of faith in popular devotionalism is the note that signals authentic evangelization, "a true expression of the spontaneous missionary activity of the people of God" (*Evangelii Gaudium* 122). He also approaches this in Marian terms, giving examples of popular devotionalism like mothers with sick children clinging to their rosaries, and "the hope poured into a candle" lit with "a prayer for help from Mary" (§125).

In this book, we will follow Francis's lead and use a classic example of Marian popular piety—the titles of Mary from the Litany of Loreto—as a lens through which to explore the relation of faith and culture in the work of evangelization. In this, we will continue to see Mary emerge as both a pattern for us to explore tilling the soil, in the sense of entering deeply into a host culture so that the gospel can truly take root within it, and sowing the seed, proclaiming the message "in all its richness" so it is not diluted or adversely affected by being fitted to the context in question. We will see the titles from Litany of Loreto as instructive hermeneutical lenses for exploring these dimensions to Mary in evangelization, for these titles will be shown both to resonate with the dynamics involved in evangelization (the "central axis"), but also to be formative for the practice of evangelizing. That is, we will see that Marian piety can form, reform, and even correct the work of evangelization, for the titles by which she is venerated promise to hold together the complex interrelation of different stimuli appropriate to diverse cultural settings. This formative potential to the veneration of Mary should be approached as an extension of Aquinas's insight that the image of God in human beings is conformed to God himself by grace as someone "actually and habitually knows and loves God."[25] For Aquinas, human beings are formed, or rather con-formed, formed *with* God, through habitually knowing and loving him. Insofar as piety is an example of habitual knowledge and love of God, then, it is involved in this work of con-formation. Drawing on this passage from the *Summa*, then, knowing and loving God through Mary has the potential to con-form the work of evangelization, to mold it, shape it, and set it on the right path for the glory of God. Analyzing Mary's titles of veneration from the Litany of Loreto, therefore, will unlock the hidden depth of the Star of Evangelization, a radiant light through which the splendor of Christ shines forth in numerous ways, appropriate to different settings, and can bear fruit in the lives of those who proclaim his name.

In what follows, the light of Christ will shine forth from the figure of Mary in ways relevant to this inquiry, each of which is discussed through one of her titles from the Litany of Loreto. Mary will be approached, first, as the "Mirror of Justice" through the writing of Pedro Arrupe, SJ. This title of Mary will be seen to resonate with Arrupe's approach to evangelization as "inculturation," for this approach commends that we evangelize by "reflecting" or "mirroring" what is just, right, and good in a specific cultural setting. Part of the work of evangelization in this approach will be to "till the soil" of a host culture, tending what is just within it. The title Mirror of Justice, however, will also reveal some reformative or corrective aspects, in that the definition of what is just in Scripture and Tradition is already affected by a specific culture, the classical culture of Greece and Rome, so Mary's title reminds us that evangelization is not always only the meeting of the gospel with a new "host" culture, but the meeting point of *two* cultures, one of which has been formed by the faith. This consideration causes the light of Christ to shine forth from a different angle, and we will explore this—through Mary's title "Seat of Wisdom"—by drawing on the work of Joseph Ratzinger, who commends an approach of "interculturality" as an alternative to inculturation. By exploring evangelization as the meeting of two cultures, Ratzinger shows how a criterion, or firm basis, is required to show how a culture formed by the gospel can change in fusing with another culture, a "seat" from which to evangelize, which he defines as "truth." Here, the emphasis moves to "sowing the seed," concentrating on the truth of Christ's message as the locus of proclaiming the faith. Of course, this approach also resonates with Mary's title Seat of Wisdom, but our discussion will consider how, in today's contemporary situation of relativism and subjectivism, the notion of "truth" is often called into question.

This consideration causes another beam of light to shine forth from Mary, which will be approached through her title "Mystical Rose." Drawing on the theology of Hans Urs von Balthasar, we will move from "truth" to "beauty," exploring evangelization through the flowering of beauty in human cultural expression, beauty as a means of communicating Christ and his Church. Discussing some of the theoretical background to von Balthasar's theology, we will see that beauty promises to hold together our dual concern of "tilling the soil" and "sowing the seed" more closely. This is, first, because he maintains that worldly, cultural beauty can function as a vessel for the beauty of Jesus Christ, so "tilling the soil" of cultural beauty is an important aspect of evangelization. But second, it is also because he maintains that beauty is objective, and thus able to communicate the truth of Christ without being undermined by subjectivism and relativism, so beauty can "sow the seed." Holding "tilling the soil" and "sowing the seed" together in this way, von Balthasar's work prima facie provides the perfect coalescing of call and response that evangelization seeks, but Mary's title Mystical Rose will again demonstrate some reformative or corrective potential, in that the rose is an ancient symbol, not only through the beauty of the flower, but also through its thorns, connected symbolically with Christ's crown of thorns. That Christ is a "sign of rejection," crowned with thorns and mocked by Roman soldiers, suggests evangelizers should also be concerned with what a culture rejects: what dominant cultural norms define as ugly or undesirable.

Our inquiry will thus continue through studying the life and work of an exemplary evangelizer who cared for those rejected by their dominant culture: Dorothy Day. Day's work in showing forth the reversal of worldly values in Christ, and its potential for proclaiming his Church, will be approached through the title of Mary, "Tower of David." Insofar as Christ's kingdom is "not from this world" (John 18:36), and David was an unarmed shepherd boy taking on the mighty Goliath, the poor and simple woman, Mary, resonates with this approach to evangelization. Analyzing this title further will reveal that David does become king and finds a way of acting with integrity in political power structures. As an "anointed" one, he highlights that the Spirit anoints the faithful to different callings in different situations, while Day's uncompromising single-mindedness is perhaps not suited to all people in all settings.

We will conclude our inquiry studying the work of John Henry Newman, whose focus on the "simple assent" of faith promises to offer a broader point of orientation for evangelizing than Dorothy Day, but who also, importantly, can hold together "tilling the soil" and "sowing the seed"—bringing us closer to the perfect coalescing of call and response that we seek. Newman reminds us that cultural sophistication can be deeply suspect in fostering a conviction that human beings can flourish without the grace of God, by encroaching on the sphere of religion. Therefore, in following Newman, we will explore "tilling the soil" as the cultivation of humility, or simplicity. Yet Newman also reminds us that the proclamation of the gospel must also be simple, in the sense of straightforward, direct, and "pure in heart" (Matt 5:8). In this way, "tilling the soil" intertwines with "sowing the seed," sowing the truth of Christ in single-minded integrity. This approach resonates with Mary's title "Tower of Ivory," for ivory is an ancient symbol of purity and simplicity, and, as we have seen, Mary's appellation as a "tower" involves the reversal of worldly expectations, in this case through humility.

In the following chapters, Mary is a cohesive key in holding together the diverse theological coordinates at work in evangelization: both making the message as understandable and persuasive as possible (tilling the soil) and preserving the faith in its untouchable purity (sowing the seed). The con-formative riches of Marian piety will also be explored in detail, showing how venerating Mary informs and reforms the life of faith. In summary, this book will show how Mary as the Star of Evangelization offers us glittering lights that are still largely untapped in their full theological luminosity, and how, through Mary, the Church can become like the bride mentioned in Isaiah, "bedecked with her jewels,"[26] meaning arrayed with the jewels of multifarious cultures combining to offer a diverse prism through which can shine the resplendent light of Christ, the light of the world.

Chapter 1

The Theological Coordinates of Culture in *Gaudium et Spes*

THE INTRODUCTION HIGHLIGHTED the imperative on all members of the Catholic Church to proclaim the gospel, and described the ambiguity attending the question of *how* this imperative should proceed. This ambiguity is undergirded by the basic dynamics of what Paul VI calls the "central axis" of evangelization: maintaining the heritage of faith in untouchable purity, while making it as understandable and persuasive as possible. The fundamentally Marian texture of these dynamics has also been laid out, for Mary is understood here as a primary locus of call and response. That is, she is the one to whom the word in all its purity goes out, and yet also the one in whom it finds its human answer or *fiat*, the place where it grows and develops humanly ("let it be with me according to your word" [Luke 1:38]). Both sides of Paul VI's "central axis" can therefore be approached through the dual-sidedness of Mary, enabling us to discern the latent possibilities inherent in her title: Star of Evangelization.

We have also begun to glimpse how Mary's dual-sidedness is indicated by some of her ancient titles in the Litany of Loreto. We will focus on these titles later to orient various strategies of evangelization. These are strategies that, on the one hand, emphasize the cultivating of a proper response *to* proclamation through concentrating on how the word can be accommodated in the sense of "fitted," seeking places where it can humanly grow and develop. Evangelization proceeds primarily by tilling the soil, tending and cultivating a host culture so the seed of the word can take root. Yet, on the other hand, we will encounter strategies that emphasize maintaining the purity of the message against dominant cultural norms, through concentrating on how the word is accommodated in the sense of genuinely "inhabiting" human hearts in its full authenticity. With this second emphasis, evangelization is focused on its uncompromising call; it proceeds by sowing the seed, proclaiming the message so it goes forth and brings new life.

Before looking at the different understandings of faith and culture at work in the theologians and witnesses to be discussed in the remaining chapters, the task, here, is to examine the key magisterial text that deals with the relation of Catholic teaching to culture, *Gaudium et Spes*. We will first discuss the definition of *culture* given explicitly in this document. This shows the essentially optimistic view of culture mentioned previously: culture as edificatory. However, as we will see, there is another approach to culture at work implicitly in *Gaudium et Spes*. This implicit approach will be seen not to approach culture as edificatory, but as essentially ambivalent—capable of exhibiting not only positive (edificatory) facets, but also negative and potentially destructive tendencies.

This discussion will present the coordinates to study theologies of culture in more detail, thus providing the requisite orientation for embarking on the work of evangelization itself, because our ability to interpret theologically the cultural expressions we meet as evangelizers will of course affect how we put Paul VI's central axis into action. That is, if culture is approached as constructively formative of human nature, then the worldviews of others will provide evangelizers with ample resources for making the message understandable and persuasive by tilling the soil, building on and extending the natural flowering of persons in their humanity. If, however, culture is essentially ambivalent and can therefore exhibit negative tendencies, in encountering unhelpful or unconstructive features, evangelizers will focus on the untouchable purity of the message by sowing the seed so that it can be imparted unsullied by these destructive influences.

As both the underlying approaches to culture function in *Gaudium et Spes*—a magisterial document with the full authority of an ecumenical council—every effort will be made to hold both together in a creative tension or polarity. Approached in this way, the positive and negative approaches to culture at work beneath the question of *how* to evangelize begin to appear as angles or coordinates that, if held in tension, cause the encounter between the light of Christ and humanity to "refract" or "prism" into a multifarious array of beams, in which the light of Christ shines differently in a broad spectrum of colors centered on the figure of Mary, in whom the Word becomes human, the *humus* where Christ is made *homo*: *homo factus est*.

DEFINING CULTURE IN
GAUDIUM ET SPES—EXPLICITLY

Most readers will know that the title *Gaudium et Spes* is shorthand for the more unwieldy full title of "The Pastoral Constitution on the Church in the Modern World." It is of course Latin for the opening words of the document, which speak of "joys and the hopes, the griefs and the anxieties of the men of this age," which is the same "the joys and hopes, the griefs and anxieties of the followers of Christ" (§1).[1] Naming the document in this way simply follows Catholic tradition of using the Latin opening words of magisterial documents as titles, but the words *Gaudium et Spes* resonate deeply with the themes and the substance of the document's teaching, which overflow with joyful optimism about the role of the Church in the postconciliar world.

This joyful anticipation is quite remarkable. The open-hearted exploration of the possibilities for "mutual upbuilding," or *aedificationis* (Rom 14:19), are even more striking when one recalls that the Church was encountering the strange new world emerging from the darkness of two world wars and their geopolitical aftermath. Perhaps we should be grateful that Catholic tradition only uses the short opening phrase for naming the document, otherwise it would bear the far more negative nouns "grief and anxiety" (*luctus et angor*), and undermine the overall sense of hopeful joy with which the document is associated in the minds of the faithful.

Despite the overarching atmosphere of hopeful joy, this chapter will expose an implicit two-sidedness in *Gaudium et Spes* pertaining to the definition of *culture* therein. For all the sanguine optimism with which the conciliar fathers tell us explicitly what culture is, the detail of the document's discussions is more doubtful—implicitly—in its evaluation of culture. In this way, we will see that not only can "webs of significance" evoke the joys and hopes of humankind, but also the grief and anxieties of the reality of human experience, and that, in sharing this grief and anxiety, the Church is called to sound a more cautious note about where things have gone wrong and to proclaim the message in all its untouchable purity, untarnished by human fallenness and sin. In short, if we approach the cultural expressions of this world in "joy and hope," we will tend to make the proclamation as understanding and persuasive as possible within the mode of expressions we meet. But if we approach the cultures of this world as indicative of the grief and anxieties of human hearts, we might ask why such sorrows pervade human experience and what resources Catholic teaching might offer to counter the causes of these sorrows.

Gaudium et Spes is in two parts, the first dealing with the Church's "teaching on man, on the world which is the enveloping context of man's existence, and on man's relations to his fellow men," and the second on "various aspects of modern life and human society," particularly "questions and problems which, in this general area, seem to have a greater urgency in our day" (preface, n. 1). One of these questions in the second part, with great urgency for the conciliar fathers, is the question of *culture*, discussed in articles 53–62. Exactly why culture was of such concern for the Council could be the subject of a lengthy discussion, but we can surmise, in brief and general terms, that the decades preceding Vatican II saw the growth of intrinsically non-Christian forms of social organization, in extreme forms like Soviet communism or fascism, and more moderately, like variants of post-Enlightenment humanism such as liberalism and secularism. To consider this period of immense change in terms of culture, we need to remember that before the Enlightenment, in the West at least, culture and Catholicism were deeply and insepa-rably intertwined in societies making up Christendom. This means the relationship between the Church and non-Christian cultures had simply not been on the agenda for centuries, and as post-Enlightenment forms of culture took hold in the nineteenth and early twentieth centuries, the magisterial lens of the Church was focused elsewhere, on the philosophi-cal bases of modernity (such as rationalism, at Vatican I), the theological accommodations of it (such as with the modernist "drama"), or the politi-cal dispositions of the Church in the wake of the Industrial Revolution (such as Leo XII's *Rerum Novarum*).[2]

The passage dealing with culture in chapter 2 of part 2 of *Gaudium et Spes*, therefore, signifies a moment in which the Church reflects on how it should understand its mission and purpose in a modern world where cul-ture can no longer be presumed to be Christian. Regarding the concerns of this book, a culture calling for evangelization will be non-Catholic, to at least some extent, and we must therefore look closely at how this authoritative magisterial document tells us we should meet the culture of the world outside the Church, or situations where "outside influences" are at work in the Church, to discern how to conduct the business of evangelization.

Bearing in mind that the seismic changes in Western culture that preceded the Council led to movements like the decadence of *Fin de siècle*, the destruction of literary and visually artistic norms in modernism, and the irreverent infantilism of Dadaism, the early twentieth century clearly pushed understandings of culture into areas very different from the "clas-sical" definition we discussed earlier. This is the definition given explicitly in *Gaudium et Spes*: "The word 'culture' in its general sense indicates every-thing whereby man develops and perfects his many bodily and spiritual qualities" (§53). One might well ask whether the cultures effective in modernity genuinely offer things "whereby man develops and perfects his many bodily and spiritual qualities" when movements like those previ-ously listed set out to challenge anything straightforwardly edificatory belonging to culture. Before responding to this question, however, let us give the Council fathers a good hearing.

It is important, first, to be aware that the joyful optimism of *Gaudium et Spes* not only pertains to the overall themes of its teaching, but also to the etymological minutiae of its wording. Therefore, the fathers interpret "culture" in the most hopeful sense of the term, which aligns comfortably with its etymological roots. As we have seen, the original Latin is *cultura*, an agricultural term pointing to culture as the development or fostering of the fruits of our humanity. The explicit definition of *culture* in *Gaudium et Spes* thus utilizes the traditional and most etymologically authentic definition of the word, as that which *edifies*: that which is tended, nurtured, and guarded as a means of bringing human nature to bear fruit. The question unavoidably arises: What are these fruits? *Gaudium et Spes* offers a direct answer: "the goods and values of nature" (§53). Nature here, of course, means not the fields and groves of the farmer, but *human* nature, that which pertains to all human beings and defines us as members of the human species. What this document explicitly understands by culture, then, is "everything whereby man develops and perfects his many bodily and spiritual qualities," namely, "the goods and values of human nature."

Of course, a completely exhaustive compendium of how such goods and values have been understood in the Western intellectual tradition is far beyond the scope of *Gaudium et Spes*, and indeed beyond the scope of this book. But we can see the fathers offering us, in article 54, an interpretation of what it terms "the culture of today" (modern culture) by listing various "goods and values" of one particular cultural domain, called— albeit in very general terms—"modern culture." The document claims that "the culture of today possesses particular characteristics," three of which we will discuss here:

> "Sciences which are called exact greatly develop critical judgment."
>
> "Historical studies make it much easier to see things in their mutable and evolutionary aspects, customs and usages are becoming more and more uniform."
>
> "The increase of commerce between the various nations and human groups opens more widely to all the treasures of different civilizations and thus little by little, there develops a more universal form of human culture, which better promotes and expresses the unity of the human race to

the degree that it preserves the particular aspects of the different civilizations."

So, bearing in mind the document's concern with culture as that which nurtures "the goods and values of nature," let us discern what values are at work here. First, we are dealing with discrimination or judgment, the ideal of perceiving the truth of the reality of things, a value sought by what St. Thomas Aquinas would call a virtue of the speculative intellect, namely, knowledge (*scientia*): "using good reasoning to arrive at the truth of the things of this world."[3] Second, *Gaudium et Spes* highlights the advent of what could be called "historical consciousness," an all-pervasive awareness of how deeply temporally situated all human endeavors are. It is a consciousness of their distinctiveness respective to their historical context. To give an example of the all-pervasiveness of historical consciousness from theological studies, consider the fact that, today, people will spontaneously and unreflectively consider Jesus as a citizen of the first century, a man of the ancient world. If one goes back before the Enlightenment, to premodern art and literature, Jesus's temporal situatedness is not a primary attribute of his identity; he is spontaneously and unreflectively approached without consideration of how different the world was in his time, and he is generally approached just as a contemporary. *Gaudium et Spes* praises the development of historical consciousness, and the value involved here can again be broadly classified as "knowing the truth of things," something sought by the virtue of *scientia*.[4] Third, we can discern in the document's comments about a "more universal form of human culture" developing, immense value being placed on acknowledging the universality of human nature, with concomitant values like fraternity and mutual respect. These values, of course, challenge divisive or elitist readings of human identity, such as those exhibited by European colonialism or the enslavement of African Americans. This newly emerging universality could also be termed "global consciousness," following hot on the heels of the "increase of commerce between the various nations and human groups," which has, in digital technology and social media, surely surpassed anything the conciliar fathers could have envisaged in the 1960s.

This universality is not only praised on its own account, but also for its apparent potential to accommodate diversity, for it "promotes and expresses the unity of the human race to the degree that it preserves the particular aspects of the different civilizations." Note, here, that this praising of diversity in unity is a direct corollary of the explicit, optimistic definition of *culture* of the preceding article (§53). That is, if culture is, *by definition*, inherently edifying, then we would want to preserve the specific characteristics of each culture, for all these cultures would involve the blossoming of the "goods and values of nature." Here, a question arises that will prove important in the following chapters, particularly when we examine the theology of culture at work in Pedro Arrupe, SJ, whose writings are a direct outworking of this paragraph in article 54. The question—very basically—involves the issue of whether each culture has specific characteristics that can be brought into harmonious interplay with the universality of Christianity. In short, do we want *all* elements of modern culture to be preserved? Or, in other words (in line with the dynamics described earlier), will all elements of modern culture enable the content of evangelization to be made as understandable and persuasive as possible, or might certain elements conflict with this content?

DEFINING CULTURE IN *GAUDIUM ET SPES*—IMPLICITLY

From the previous section, it could safely be assumed that the possibility that modern culture might exhibit negative, unconstructive, or inimical elements simply does not come on the agenda for the writers of *Gaudium et Spes*, who state clearly that the cultural is the edifying, that which refines and develops human nature. For this reason, it is even more surprising that, while the document celebrates "the birth of a new humanism" in article 55, it goes on, in article 56, to describe modern culture in ways that suggest the lens of joy and hope has gone somewhat askew. This article highlights the "difficulties and duties" involved in the relation of the Church to the modern world, setting out certain dangers that align to the positive commendations provided in article 54. Let us consider three of these that align to the three positive (value-related) characteristics of modern culture previously listed:

"How can we quickly and progressively harmonize the proliferation of particular branches of study with the necessity of forming a synthesis of them, and of preserving among men the faculties of contemplation and observation which lead to wisdom?"

"How is the dynamism and expansion of a new culture to be fostered without losing a living fidelity to the heritage of tradition?"

"What is to be done to prevent the increased exchanges between cultures…from disturbing the life of communities, from destroying the wisdom received from ancestors, or from placing in danger the character proper to each people?"

In the first of these, we can see that the value of perceiving the truth of the reality of things, connected with the virtue of *scientia*, threatens not only to lead to a fragmentation of entrenched academic specialization, but also threatens to cultivate such mastery over the world that God's creation is no longer met with wonder, but as an opportunity for human-centered manipulation and control. Consequently, the development of one virtue (*scientia*) threatens to drown out another, namely "wisdom" or what tradition calls *sapientia*, defined by Thomas as the "use of right reason concerning God."[5] A note of caution is thus sounded about the danger of human powers of discrimination and judgement, which, in their apparently limitless potential for exactitude, might cause us to lose sight of their rootedness in God, and of the genuinely limitless source of all, the "Author of life" (Acts 3:15).

In the second note of caution, there is an implication that the emergence of historical consciousness, which is based on linear notions of progressive development, threatens to lead to an overconfident sense of contemporary superiority over the allegedly more primitive past. This can arguably be seen in today's fetishization of the "new," where gadgets like smartphones and tablets are in an ever-accelerating cycle of being upgraded or replaced. A sense of superiority over the past is, of course, a neuralgic issue for Catholic thought, which prizes the "heritage of tradition"—the gradual accumulation of sedimented teaching and praxis that grows through the collective contributions of the ages—and therefore depends inextricably on the insights of our foregoers. An example of how a dependence on traditional wisdom is an issue for culture, and not just theology, is seen in the writings of the eighteenth-century English philosopher Edmund Burke. Being disturbed by certain elements of the Enlightenment, Burke highlighted that "reason" (which is related to *scientia*) is essentially a "private" affair, something self-enclosed, which he considers part of the "private stock" of individuals. He argues that rather than relying solely on one's own reason, "individuals would do better to avail themselves of the general bank and capital of nations and of ages," employing "their sagacity" to depend on the "latent wisdom" of tradition.[6] As our cultural traditions are storehouses of this latent wisdom, we can again consider this note of caution to be pointing us toward the danger of *sapientia* being dwarfed by *scientia*, of our too self-assured confidence in our current perceptions of reality drowning out the accumulated fruits of our predecessors.

In the third note of caution, this same concern with tradition is still at play, and is added to by geographical concerns. The values of universality, fraternity, and mutual respect might threaten genuine diversity, drowning out the distinctiveness of different communities in a "one-size-fits-all" identity, "placing in danger the character proper to each people." That is, although this new universality is praised for having the potential to incorporate different identities in diversity, this is by no means assured, and *Gaudium et Spes* considers it a genuine danger that a particularly dominant culture will define the contours of the universal, in which the norms of one people are unwarrantedly imposed on others to the detriment of their authentic difference.

In these three examples, therefore, *Gaudium et Spes* maintains there are "difficulties" attending modern culture. If we are to take "culture" in the strict sense as that which edifies, then these difficulties or potential dangers would be those that do not belong to culture proper, but are somehow "uncultured" or inauthentically human, pertaining to what would often be termed (albeit in rather extreme-sounding parlance) "barbarism." However, the wording of *Gaudium et Spes* makes it difficult to offset the cultural and the barbaric in any straightforward fashion. Article 57 does tell us that the "unfortunate results" of modernity "do not necessarily follow from the culture of today," which seems to point toward negative facets as "uncultured" or barbaric, but this sentence goes on to state that these drawbacks should not "lead us into the temptation of not acknowledging its positive values" (§57). This reference to "positive values" seems to imply that there are also negative aspects, and therefore culture is not only that which edifies, builds up, or cultivates the goods and values of nature like a farmer tending his crops. If culture has positive values, this implies culture can exhibit negative facets, and that culture itself is something at least relatively ambivalent. If culture is merely what cultivates "the goods and values of nature," how can it then present "unfortunate results" that threaten to inhibit or even negate these values? The question of whether these drawbacks are a direct consequence of culture itself is left open, and consequently, there is a certain dissonance in this chapter of *Gaudium et Spes*, a dissonance between culture as the inherently edifying, on the one hand, and as something morally ambivalent, on the other. Indeed, this dissonance demonstrates that there is an implicit suggestion that there is more to this term *culture* than meets the eye in the explicit definition of article 53.

A two-sidedness of positive values and negative aspects to "the culture of today" is, of course, close to the pedestrian English use of the word, which is not necessarily bound to goodness or edification. Those familiar with the more pedestrian sense of the term may even be surprised to learn that originally it means "that which edifies" or "builds up" the goods and values of human nature. The word is indeed still often used in a much more neutral sense, like what we find in T. S. Eliot's *Notes towards a Definition of Culture*: "the term culture…includes all the characteristic activities and interests of a people."[7] We see, therefore, an ambiguity in the English word *culture*, which can mean that which edifies, like *Gaudium et Spes* article 53, or something neutral, like the "characteristic activities and interests of a people." As *Gaudium et Spes* implies, there are positive and negative sides to "modern culture." Similar ambiguity is implied in the document itself, between culture as that which edifies, and culture as merely the characteristic activities of a people, which can work for either good or ill.

If we look elsewhere in the document, the suggestion that the term *modern culture* means more than simply that which builds up the goods and values of human nature in the modern world, is confirmed by the moments where the document makes unflinching statements about human sinfulness. If the cultural is the human, as we have seen, and the human story is heavily characterized by sin, surely this means sin affects culture, that culture does not always garner the proper fruits of human nature. This would be a fair inference to make from statements such as the following: "A monumental struggle against the powers of darkness pervades the whole history of man. The battle was joined from the very origins of the world and will continue until the last day, as the Lord has attested" (§37). Quoting Romans 12:2:"Be not conformed to this world," the article defines *world* as meaning "spirit of vanity and malice which transforms into an instrument of sin those human energies intended for the service of God and man." Of course, if this spirit of vanity and malice distorts the quintessentially human business of culture, culture is not merely that which edifies, but it is enmeshed in the full complexity of human moral obscurity.

Moreover, in discussing the introductory statement, "The Situation of Men in the Modern World," we read, "Growing numbers of people are abandoning religion in practice." And furthermore, "unlike former days, the denial of God or of religion, or the abandonment of them, are no longer unusual and individual occurrences. For today it is not rare for such things to be presented as requirements of scientific progress or of a certain new humanism" (§7). This development is not viewed as something edifying and worthy of cultivation, but as something disturbing. But if it is unedifying and unsettling, it is surprising given the explicit definition of culture in article 53, where the "new humanism" is also connected by the fathers with the expressions of modern culture. It states that "these views…influence literature, the arts, the interpretation of the humanities and of history and civil laws" (§7). Furthermore, in discussing atheism, the document speaks of "those poisonous doctrines and actions which contradict reason and the common experience of humanity, and dethrone man from his native excellence" (§21).[8] We might well ask, here, if teachings and ways of acting can ever be entirely *extra*-cultural (in the neutral use of the term), or if we might have to guard *against* certain forms of culture in the work of evangelization as having little or no capacity to edify? Recall the opening words of *Gaudium et Spes*, the claim that "the joys and the hopes, the griefs and the anxieties of the men of this age" are the same "joys and hopes, the griefs and anxieties of the followers of Christ." As indicated earlier, if culture is understood in an ambivalent sense, as mere "characteristic activities" in sharing the "griefs and anxieties" of the world, might not evangelization take the form of challenging the root of those sorrows? More specifically, sharing the griefs and anxieties caused by "systematic" atheism, a grief and anxiety bearing on human life stripped of awareness of its divine purpose in an explicit rejection of God and a refusal of the possibility of unending joy in Christ, would surely call for members of the Body of Christ to challenge those presuppositions, to declare "in untouchable purity" (*Evangelii Nuntiandi* 3) that "from him and through him and to him are all things" (Rom 11:36).

It is, therefore, unavoidable to conclude that *Gaudium et Spes* approaches culture not only with the explicit definition of article 53, but also implicitly as something capable of both positive and negative expressions. How we classify the cultural expressions with the explicit and implicit definitions at work in *Gaudium et Spes* will, of course, define exactly how Paul VI's central axis will bear on the living fruit of evangelization—the proclamation of Christ and his Church. If culture is that which edifies, an evangelizer will seek to find points of contact or resonances in the culture of an addressee, to "fit" the message to terms the addressee can appreciate: making the content understandable and persuasive. If culture is evaluated negatively, an evangelizer will challenge the dominant norms, ensuring the content can be transmitted authentically and without unwelcome intrusions: proclaiming the message in its "untouchable purity."

THE COORDINATES AS CREATIVE TENSION

The theological coordinates of culture in *Gaudium et Spes* point to two different approaches to modern culture, indicating that there are two sides to the theology of Vatican II. Indeed, it is tempting here to classify this dual-sidedness as a split between the two factions usually classified as "liberal" or "progressive," on the one hand, and "traditionalist" or "conservative," on the other. Those in the liberal/progressive camp would, of course, be expected to take a more positive view of modern culture, and those of a traditionalist/conservative bent, a more critical and countercultural outlook.[9] However, to approach this dual-sidedness as a binary split—as something mutually exclusive—would challenge the basic tenets of this book, that there are multifarious expressions of Catholic teaching that can and do enunciate Christ and his Church differently in various contexts, with the figure of Mary as a point of coherence. It is, therefore, fitting for us not to condemn one set of coordinates and opt for the other, but rather to hold them together in a creative tension. This is intended to move toward more nonbinary interpretations of the Council, classically stated by Pope Benedict XVI as a "hermeneutic of continuity" over against "hermeneutics of discontinuity and rupture." Consequently, the optimism and positivity of the explicit definition of *culture* in article 53, as applied to "modern culture," is seen not as a rupture with the tradition, ushering in completely unchartered theological territory, but as a "reform": a dynamic renewal of the wisdom inherent in the tradition bringing to light latent and, hitherto, neglected elements. Moreover, the caution and criticism of the implicit definition at work in article 56 would equally be seen, not as a retrograde or reactionary point of resistance from those who see the Church being led by the Council into dubious and undesirable teachings, but, again, as a part of the reform, interplaying with the newly emphasized dynamic elements with a stabilizing counterpoint.

This section outlines the background to the two sets of coordinates at work in *Gaudium et Spes*, to show how—on this issue of the relation of the Church to culture—we find a particularly apposite example of the benefits of approaching the Council in a nonbinary pattern, as reform within tradition, and that doing so opens the latent possibilities inherent in Mary's title, Star of Evangelization.

It is easy to discern how the ruptured or binary interpretations of Vatican II arose, particularly as *Gaudium et Spes* is a document venturing into unchartered realms: a pastoral constitution dealing with the relationship between the Church and a world threatening to become post-Christian. Because this broad concern with the "modern world" is not tied to a specific dogmatic locus, like *Dei Verbum* is tied to Scripture or *Lumen Gentium* to ecclesiology, some criticized the document as haphazard and eclectic, a "Noah's Ark" for the elements the Council could not fit into other promulgations.[10] Indeed, the fact that we are dealing with new territory, here, also explains the long-winded and, at times, highly strained process of composing the document. Examining this process enables us to discern how the two sets of coordinates in question began to emerge as a site of specific contention. As early as September 1963, a "tension was discovered" in an earlier draft, between "the Church as a heavenly structure founded on the word of God, on the one hand, and the world which is developing, growing together and seeking true justice on the other."[11] Of course, if we emphasize the Church as an otherworldly "heavenly structure," the relation to modern culture will be critically countercultural, and evangelization will focus on sowing the seed and the "untouchable purity" of the message, but if we emphasize the world as growing toward "true justice," evangelization will focus on tilling the soil to make the message "understandable and persuasive" by building on the world's constructive tendencies so that the gospel can take root.

This tension continues to feature in the preliminary discussions, as witnessed in Zurich in 1964, when the fathers highlighted two "dangers" that could arise from overemphasizing one element at the expense of the other. The first of these dangers is described by Charles Moeller as arising from "seeing only a purely gospel-centered aspect, in accordance with which the Church would have to renounce all support from the earthly order." This would unfold into a mode of evangelizing that so emphasizes the untouchable purity of the message that it cannot make sense and be properly understood, so there is no "good soil" for it to find a home within the worldviews of its addressees. Or, put differently, "an exaggerated gospel-centeredness runs the risk that the witness which the Church has to bear the world would not be heard at all."[12] The second, opposite danger arises from "clinging too much to given historical situations," which would unfold into a mode of evangelizing whereby making the message as understandable and persuasive as possible threatens to dilute it within a specific context, so the seed of the Word itself is undermined. Indeed, the depth of this tension is indicated by the fact that these discussions are said to have featured an "incessant swing between a too exclusively gospel-centered outlook and another which was more concerned with the concrete situations in which the Church actually has to live."[13]

At Ariccia, in 1965, this tension is linked particularly with the drafting of the articles on culture. The earlier drafts of the text were criticized for being "too idyllic" in their assessment of modern culture, and not fully capturing its "tensions and antinomies." But, for Moeller at least, the depth of these tensions does not undermine the value or worth of this section of the document. He states that "the dialectical tension" at work in these discussions "contributed to enrich the text which finally became one of the most important in the whole Pastoral Constitution," even if it "had been regarded as one of the most difficult ever to be dealt with by a Council."[14] This was so difficult precisely because of the tension between the Church as world-affirming, or world-criticizing, between seeing the proclamation of the Church as seeking points that would make it understandable and persuasive, *or* as focusing on its untouchable purity. The final promulgation of the document thus strikes a "balance," or a "consensus" between these "two main tendencies," further described by Moeller as "a concrete outlook marked by a certain fundamental optimism" *and* "a dialectical, paradoxical attitude insisting on the polyvalency of the world in which the Church lives."[15]

This tension is indicated by many of the revisions that have left us with wording of the text as discussed earlier. To give one example, let us take the passage from article 55 that works from the optimistic, positive view of culture as edificatory to argue for "the duty imposed on us [i.e., the Church] to build up a better world of truth and justice."[16] To evangelize in accordance with passages like this would mean not only seeking resonances in the worldviews of others, places where "truth and justice" are flowering, but perhaps even evangelizing by merely working for these concerns, working for a more just world. This interpretation, however, threatens to remove the content of evangelization, to jeopardize the distinctiveness of the gospel message and make evangelization indistinguishable from social and political action. For precisely this reason, it was decided to speak of a "better" (*meliorum*) world, to correct what was originally phrased a "new" (*novum*) world of truth and justice.[17] The terminology of a "new world" (cf. Rev 21:1) was removed precisely because it was thought to belong "to the eschatological terminology of Holy Scripture,"[18] and therefore to bespeak possibilities for fulfillment lying outside the purely cultural domain. The issue is this, therefore: If modern culture is independently and autonomously creating a "new world," then what is the place of the gospel and its proclamation? For reasons such as these, efforts were made to hold in tension the fact that, on the one hand, culture "needs 'grace'—and cannot thus build up a genuinely '*new* world' as spoken of in the Scriptures on its own—because it only finds its own fulfilment in grace." On the other hand, however, "grace also calls for culture, because this constitutes the normal point of insertion of grace in human life."[19]

Consequently, rather than offset one approach to culture against the other, and follow a ruptured and binary interpretation of the Council, these two approaches provide sets of coordinates that are both necessary and mutually complementary. In this, we can stand with Dondeyne, who argued that overplaying either optimism or pessimism would be a "flight from harsh reality," and therefore it is "only by having the courage to place oneself in the midst of these contradictions can we meet the cultural task of the present day."[20] Indeed, to rupture one approach from the other would severely delimit our understanding of evangelizing, which must surely work with both coordinates, emphasized in a balance respective of the needs of a specific context. Holding these coordinates together is thus advantageous, a perspective that mirrors Moeller's statement about the entire document, which, he states, "lost a little of its homogeneity" in the complex process of balancing its tensions, but by doing so "gained in wealth of context and complexity."[21]

Importantly, the preliminary discussions for the document linked the coordinates involved in relating the Church to modern culture directly with evangelization, and this link made it into the final text, with a note highlighting the statement made by Pope Pius IX: "one must never lose sight of the fact that the Church's objective is to evangelize, not to civilize. If it does civilize, it is done through evangelizing."[22] In this sense, the document is clear: the Church carries out its mission, and in that very act it "stimulates and advances human and civic culture" (*Gaudium et Spes* 58). Holding the two approaches to culture in *Gaudium et Spes* together, and drawing on this statement by Pius IX, we can see how we gain a wealth of complexity. That is, evangelization can proceed by civilizing, but it need not always civilize, insofar as it might involve challenging the cultural norms that dictate what is considered civil in certain contexts.

Gaudium et Spes holds that, while culture is that which edifies (see §53), it can slip into negative and destructive tendencies, or what would be termed "barbarism." In seeking to hold these two coordinates together, as indeed is required by the magisterial authority of the document, certain possibilities that are perhaps strange and unexpected become evident. For example, it would seem from the foregoing analysis that even edificatory elements of culture can slip into barbarism. That is, the cultural is that which fosters the flowering of humanity, but this flowering can—conversely and even paradoxically—inhibit the fulfillment of this flowering in the person of Jesus. Moreover, this would seem to suggest that some values of human nature, appearing prima facie to be something positive and worthy of being celebrated and cultivated, might in fact be somewhat dangerous, notwithstanding their apparent rectitude, and should therefore be treated with caution. Indeed, in extreme cases, we might find that we must evangelize by challenging the norms of the "civilized." However, of course, some of the values of culture must be straightforwardly edificatory, and in such cases, we can evangelize by civilizing.

Applying Paul VI's "central axis," we have so far considered cultural expressions either positively or negatively. In positive contexts, evangelization would proceed by emphasizing making the message understandable and persuasive, or in negative contexts, by concentrating on imparting the message in its untouchable purity. However, holding the two coordinates of the approach to culture in *Gaudium et Spes* together in a creative tension renders our field of vision significantly more complex. In particularly positive contexts, we could build on the values of a host culture to encourage them to find their fulfillment in Christ. We will explore this possibility in the next chapter through the work of Pedro Arrupe, SJ.

Chapter 2

Inculturation

Mary as "Mirror of Justice"

HAVING DISCERNED THE THEOLOGICAL coordinates, we can now embark on a focused reading of a theology of culture to bring out its corresponding strategy of evangelization: Pedro Arrupe's approach to inculturation. In this chapter, we focus on one of the beams of the prism of the light of Christ that refracts from holding the coordinates of *Gaudium et Spes* in tension. This beam concerns evangelizing by *tilling the soil* of culture. Inculturation focuses on the response to evangelization by its addressees, on the proclamation making sense and being understood in terms of the worldview of its hearers. It does this by considering that Christ can be incarnated in any cultural setting—brought to birth in such a way that he genuinely belongs to that culture, expressing its inner values and bringing them to fulfillment. This, in turn, presupposes that the gospel is essentially transcendent to culture, thereby enabling it to flower in any culture, and that there are "seeds of the Word" (*semina Verbi*) in cultures prior to evangelization, so Christ is always present latently within human cultural expression.

This chapter uncovers some difficulties with inculturation, leading from the foregoing analysis of *Gaudium et Spes*, which presents certain conditions for evangelizing, incumbent particularly on tilling the soil. This is demonstrated by Pius IX's comment that "the Church's objective is to evangelize, not to civilize. If it does civilize, it is done through evangelizing."[1] The Church's mission, therefore, is the proclamation of sacramental life in Christ, and we should not lose sight of this mission by so emphasizing the nurturing of cultural values that the message, itself, loses its force. From this perspective, cultural development or upbuilding must follow *from* evangelization, and not the other way round: "the Church, *in the very fulfillment of her own function*, stimulates and advances human and civic culture" (§58).[2] Because inculturation considers all cultures to have values that can find their fulfillment in Christ, the boundary between civilizing and evangelizing is threatened because the cultivation of value alone, for Arrupe, seems to lead to Christ himself, as if Christ himself lay dormant within the goods and values of human nature.

A similar point is demonstrated secondly by the change of terminology made to *Gaudium et Spes* in highlighting "the duty which is imposed upon us, that we build a better [*meliorum*] world based upon truth and justice" (§55). By opting for a "better" (*meliorum*) world over against what was originally phrased a "new" (*novum*) world, a clear distinction is made between a culture fulfilled by the gospel, and one being fulfilled autonomously by purely human means. This editorial decision was based on the conviction that, without the grace of Christ, the pursuit of justice will not triumph over sin, it will not bring humanity to fulfillment, and will not, therefore, build a world that is genuinely *new* in the scriptural meaning of the term. The distinction between *meliorum* and *novum* provides a further dimension to the condition for evangelizing by tilling the soil of a host culture. Namely, care must be taken to ensure that the stimulation and advancement of human and civic culture by the Church is not mistaken for an end in itself. It must, therefore, be kept in mind that the cultivation of values is only a means to create a *better* world, and not the *new* world of the gospel.

In what follows, the advantageousness of approaching these theological dynamics through Mary as the Star of Evangelization will begin to bear fruit. One of the titles from the Litany of Loreto proves itself particularly helpful for understanding the tilling of cultural soil with Arrupe's approach of inculturation: the "Mirror of Justice." Inculturation involves the conviction that Christ is at work in the edificatory values of all human cultures, and so evangelizing through inculturation will involve finding and nurturing those values as "resonances" or "points of contact" where the gospel proclamation can be rightly heard. But our analysis of *Gaudium et Spes* shows that every care must be taken to ensure the cultivation of these values does not become an end in itself, that our mission does not become mere civilizing, and that it is ever borne in mind, therefore, that purely human cultural values can only create a better world and not the truly *novum* life in Christ. It is regarding precisely these conditions that the title of Mary comes into its own.

In what follows, we will discern that the value of justice, considered centrally important by Arrupe, cannot be fully disentangled from some of its cultural elements rooted in Greco-Roman, classical culture. Consequently, classical culture is particularly important to the Christian proclamation, and therefore, Arrupe's conviction that the gospel of Christ is transcendent to culture stands in need of modification. This occurs when we understand our tilling of the soil as a "mirroring of justice," finding resonances in a cultural setting on the condition that these values genuinely reflect ("mirror") the understanding of justice in Scripture and Tradition, which is unavoidably intertwined with the classical background.

The significance of the classical heritage for the Catholic tradition has long been recognized, stemming originally from the Church fathers, who called it "a preparation for the gospel" (*praeparatio evangelica*). This nomenclature is based on the view that the ground for the spread of Christianity across the ancient world was prepared (or "tilled") by classical thought, enabling the gospel message to take root. By approaching the tilling of cultural soil through inculturation as "mirroring justice," we find a second dimension to Mary's title that serves as a corrective to Arrupe. A cultural setting of evangelization can serve as a preparatory ground for the proclamation of the gospel, but this differs importantly from considering Christ himself to be present latently in all cultural settings as "seeds of the Word." For this reason, we will draw further on Mary's title as Mirror of Justice to approach tilling the soil through inculturation only as *mirroring* Christ himself—something exemplified in Mary—and therefore making a firm distinction between tilling the soil (preparing the ground) and sowing the seed (or seeds of the Word).

PEDRO ARRUPE

Pedro Arrupe, SJ (1907–91) was the twenty-eighth superior general of the Society of Jesus (Jesuit Order).[3] He was born in the Basque region of Spain in 1907 and entered the Jesuits in 1927. During the Spanish Civil War, the Jesuits were expelled from Spain, so he trained in Belgium, Holland, and the United States. After ordination, he worked as a missionary in Japan. His task was evangelizing a culture largely untouched by the Catholic faith, where the language, art, and way of life was vastly different from that of his European homeland. Moreover, Japan in the 1930s had become increasingly aggressive on the world stage and more authoritarian at home. After the bombing of Pearl Harbor in 1941, Arrupe—a Westerner—was viewed with suspicion. He was arrested for espionage and placed in solitary confinement in prison. This was, of course, immensely challenging, and he spoke of his sorrow at being deprived of the Eucharist. Nonetheless, he experienced a particular grace at Christmas in 1941 after he heard some people whispering outside his cell. Although he initially thought people might be coming to execute him, to his amazement they burst into song and sang a Christmas carol. He then realized these were people to whom he had previously proclaimed the gospel of Christ, Japanese recipients of his missionary work, and they had come to comfort him by singing some of the songs he had taught them through the heavy and impenetrable door of his prison cell.

Arrupe was released shortly after this incident, and then lived in the Nagatsuka district on the outskirts of Hiroshima. He worked in this city as the master of novices for the Japanese Mission. He was there on August 6, 1945, the moment when the name Hiroshima became synonymous with the dropping of an atomic bomb by the US military. This occurred at 8:15 a.m. on the same date, perversely, as the Feast of the Transfiguration of Christ. Eighty thousand people were killed immediately, and in the devastation of the radioactive aftermath, the death toll was to reach around 166,000. Arrupe had heard the US B29 bomber flying over the city, but he was used to the air raid sirens and so he carried on with his business unalarmed. Shortly afterward, however, there was an immense explosion, and the doors and windows of the Jesuit residence were blown in. Arrupe and his Jesuit colleagues went outside to investigate, and later recorded that as they looked out on the city from the hillside, they saw it turn into a vast lake of fire. Rather than run to safety and hide, Arrupe and his coworkers did what they could to tend the victims, giving aid to 150 injured victims, only one of whom went on to die.

Some years after this experience, Arrupe was stationed in Latin America, where he developed the deep love for the poor that character-izes his spirituality. He was elected Superior General of the Society of Jesus in 1965, and held this post until 1983, after suffering a stroke in 1981. He died ten years later in 1991.

INCULTURATION AND THE JESUIT CHARISM

Defining Inculturation

As superior general between 1965 and 1981, Arrupe had the task of leading the Jesuits through the upheavals of the period of renewal fol-lowing Vatican II. This was a time of change for the Church, and his Order was, of course, no exception. The main work of the Jesuits is codi-fied and discussed at the General Congregation that takes place every ten years. The Thirty-First General Congregation was conducted while the Council was still in session, in 1965. When the Thirty-Second Congre-gation came around, between December 2, 1974, and March 7, 1975, the Church seemed rather different from the previous Congregation of 1965. Arrupe had the task of steering his Order through this time of transition, reaping the theological fruits of Vatican II specifically in relation to the Jesuit charism.

Arrupe claims the notion of inculturation was "born" at the Thirty-Second Congregation,[4] and it is clearly therefore a response to the changes wrought by the Council. He recounts that, when the Jesuits had met in 1965, the common language was Latin, but by the time of the Thirty-Second Congregation, the Jesuits were speaking in their respective ver-naculars, so there was a plethora of tongues in use. Before the Council, the Jesuits had conducted their business in the then *lingua franca* of the Church, a language intrinsically linked with the Greco-Latin cultural heritage of

Catholicism. Now they were operating in a situation of deep plurality, with numerous languages in use, indicating that the classical culture no longer assumed supreme place. For this reason, as we will explore in the next section, those (like Arrupe) who were engaged in the mission of evangelizing needed to outline a corresponding method for evangelizing that did not assume the same centrality for the Greco-Latin heritage that was regnant before the Council.

The word *inculturation* is closely related to two other words, from which it originally derives. Both originate from cultural anthropology. The first, *enculturation*, usually refers to the process by which a child learns the rudiments of acceptable social behavior to function in their own culture, or the process by which someone encountering a new culture undergoes "the process of socialization into that new culture,"[5] learning the way of thinking, the manners and the language, and so on, of that setting. The prefix *en-* derives from a Greek preposition meaning "in,"—becoming cultured *in* a specific culture. The second related word is *acculturation*. This refers to the contact between two cultures, and more specifically, the changes that result in each. The prefix *a-* derives from the Latin *ad* meaning "to" or "toward"—cultures being altered or adjusted *to* one another, becoming acculturated to each other.

Inculturation arose originally in a theological context, and is intrinsically related to evangelization. For this reason, neither *acculturation* nor *enculturation* would suffice. *Acculturation* presupposes two distinct cultures, but with evangelization there must be some sense that the gospel is not merely a culture. Moreover, the gospel makes universal claims to truth, and so would not be expected haphazardly to acculturate itself to any circumstances. The word *inculturation* was thus coined, referring to the process by which the gospel enters (or is "inserted") into a host culture without undermining its own integrity. Etymologically, it is very similar to *enculturation*, as the prefix *in-* of *inculturation* also derives from the Greek *en-*. But, the crucial difference, here, is that with enculturation, a child learning the rudiments of social behavior, or someone immersing him- or herself in the culture of an alien people, are not seeking to alter the culture being encountered. With evangelization, however, a determinate message is being brought—Christ and his Church—and this is not encultured by evangelization, but *incarnated*. We will see further connections between incarnation and inculturation, but for now, note that the *in-* of *inculturation* should be linked with the *in-* of *incarnation*, for this is intrinsic to its meaning.

Arrupe gave a definition of *inculturation* that has since been regarded as classic. He writes,

> The fundamental and valid principle is that inculturation is the incarnation of Christian life and of the Christian message in a particular cultural context, in such a way that this experience not only finds expression through elements proper to the culture in question (this alone would be no more than a superficial adaptation), but becomes a principle that animates, directs and unifies the culture, transforming and remaking it so as to bring about a "new creation."
>
> In every case, this Christian experience is that of the People of God, that lives in a definite cultural space and has assimilated the traditional values of its own culture, but is open to other cultures.[6]

Inculturation thus means the incarnation, the bringing to birth, of "the Christian life" in terms of a host culture. But it is more than simply adorning this life with new cultural forms; the Christian life is not simply dressed up in new forms of expression, like, for example, translating the Scriptures into a new language, or changing the style of music of the liturgy. Rather, this life is disclosed as the center of a host culture—the way a culture understands the world is shown to be rooted in Christ and to find its fulfillment in him. For Arrupe, all culture is thus, in a sense, directed to Christ. The link between incarnation and inculturation proves important here, for this is not merely about bringing Christ to birth through evangelization, but is deeply linked with Christ's becoming human. Arrupe presupposes that culture forms us in our humanity: it nurtures our humanness. If we are genuinely or authentically human, and Christ is perfect humanity, then Christ will be glimpsed in the flowering of our humanity. Because Christ is archetypal humanity—the fullness of being human—the cultivation of humanity is naturally interrelated with his person.

It is easy to discern that Arrupe is drawing, here, on the explicit definition of *culture* found in article 53 of *Gaudium et Spes*. His view of culture is that it is inherently edifying, that which cultivates the "goods and values" of human nature. Focusing exclusively on this approach to culture leads to his incarnational view of evangelization, for Christ is the fulfillment of these values, "through whom all goodness comes," and to whom all that is good points. As noted earlier, Arrupe also seems to be fleshing out a specific statement from article 54 of *Gaudium et Spes*, which praises the emerging universality of modern culture. This universality is applauded for its apparent potential to accommodate diversity, for "through it the unity of mankind is being fostered and expressed in the measure that the particular characteristics of each culture are preserved." Again, this praising of diversity in unity is a direct corollary of the explicit, optimistic, definition of *culture* of the preceding article (§53). That is, if culture is, *by definition*, inherently edifying, then we would want to preserve the specific characteristics of each culture, for all these cultures would involve the blossoming of the "goods and values of nature." Moreover, the incarnational character of this can be discerned insofar as Christ is the universal human being, the Redeemer of all and universal Savior.

Inculturation and the Jesuit Mission

Before we examine inculturation more critically, it is important to situate it in the context of the Jesuit charism. The first thing to bear in mind is the deeply global nature of the Jesuit Order, which is the largest single order of priests and religious in the Catholic Church, spread over 112 nations and six continents. Consequently, there is much cultural diversity within the Order itself, as well as in the vast range of contexts in which it works. This calls to mind Arrupe's comments regarding the Thirty-Second General Congregation (where the term *inculturation* was "born"). Because the Jesuits no longer had a common tongue, he felt the Congregation involved "the experience of a deep-rooted oneness at the heart of a wide-ranging Society; never had there been such diversity in a Jesuit assembly before, never such a problem of language." He does not view this linguistic diversity negatively, however, for "there was real communication, seemingly effortless because of the overwhelming consciousness of belonging together."[7] The Congregation, therefore, uncovered a layer of belonging among the Jesuits that seemed to transcend culture, and is obviously rooted ultimately in the gospel of Jesus Christ.

Arrupe also grounds his approach in the earliest days of the Order. He does this, first, by quoting one of St. Ignatius's maxims: *Non cohiberi a maximo, contineri tamen a minimo, divinum est.* This is difficult to translate, but we could understand it as, "Not to renounce the greatest, but be concerned with the least, is holiness." Arrupe defines this maxim specifically in terms of inculturation, saying it "challenges us to hold on to the concrete and particular, even to the last cultural detail, but without renouncing the breadth and universality of those human values which no culture, nor the totality of them all, can assimilate and incarnate in [a] perfect and exhaustive way."[8] By this, Arrupe means the task of an "inculturator" is to focus attention on the specific circumstances of the cultural context in question—however lowly and unpromising—by being fully attentive to the work of human beings expressing themselves in that context, that is, to see human nature at work and locate the "goods and values" being cultivated by those people. Yet, in doing so, the evangelizer is commended not to surrender to the particular, and certainly not to surrender to anything like relativism. Rather, he or she should trust that, in this specific context genuinely universal human values can be disclosed, values that perhaps might not be disclosed in quite the same way in any other context.

A second location of inculturation in the Jesuit charism is given by Arrupe in his reference to the Spiritual Exercises. The Spiritual Exercises—originating, of course, with St. Ignatius himself—are at the center of Ignatian life and involve an extensive thirty-day immersion in the mysteries of the gospel that all Jesuits undertake. In the Second Week of the Four-Week cycle, under the "Infancy Contemplations"— meditations on the birth of Christ and the mysteries of the incarnation— the retreatant is encouraged to enter into the mystery of Jesus's birth, first by envisioning the three Divine Persons of the Blessed Trinity looking down "upon the face and circuit of the world, filled with people, and how on seeing that all were going down to Hell, they decreed in their eternity that the Second Person would become human to save the human race."[9] In this process, Ignatius commends his followers to see in turn the various persons: first, those on the face of the earth, in all their diversity of dress and appearance, some white and some black, some in peace and others at war, some weeping and others laughing, some healthy, others sick, some being born and others dying, etc.; secondly, see and consider the three Divine Persons as though on the royal seat or throne of the Divine majesty, how they look down upon the face and circuit of the world and on all its people, living in blindness, going to their death and descending into Hell; thirdly, to see our Lady and the Angel who greets her.[10]

By highlighting this Spiritual Exercise, Arrupe is clearly drawing a parallel between the evangelizing culture of an inculturator and that of the incarnation of Jesus, that is, being for all people in all times and places.

In the following Exercise, the retreatant is commended to "hear what the persons on the face of the earth are saying—the way they talk to each other and how they swear and blaspheme, etc."[11] Arrupe does not himself mention this exercise, but in "those on the face of the earth," we can envisage something analogous to all the different cultural expressions of humanity, the products of the "webs of significance" through which or to which an evangelizer must speak, "in all their diversity of dress and appearance." However, it might also be asked, here, if this description of all those on the face of the earth is fully congruent with Arrupe's optimistic view of culture based on article 53 of *Gaudium et Spes*. That is, human life in all its complexity and moral ambiguity is not necessarily viewed as intrinsically cultivating the "goods and values" of human nature, but he envisages the retreatant to hear the "swearing and blaspheming" of human beings on earth, and look at their actions, giving the example of "killing."

EVALUATING INCULTURATION

Arrupe's Witness as Evangelizer

Before investigating some of the potential difficulties with inculturation alluded to earlier, let us highlight its positive aspects or strengths.

The foregoing discussion enables us to envisage how inculturation might work within specific cultural contexts, that is, inculturation as an answer to the question *how* to evangelize culture: by being attentive and responsive to one's cultural circumstances. This attentiveness is aimed at discerning how Christ could take shape (or "incarnate") *in terms of* that host culture, taking form within the values proper to it, showing himself as that culture's fulfillment, the answer to its inward yearning. In this way, Christ can "animate, direct and unify the culture, transforming and remaking it so as to bring about a 'new creation.'" Indeed, Arrupe, is a fine example of one who tills the soil, an approach focused on the response to the call, or what Ratzinger describes as our becoming "waiting, inwardly recollected people who in the depth of prayer, longing, and faith give the Word room to grow."[12]

Pedro Arrupe not only offered an exemplary personal witness of charity to the people he served, many of whom were in abject poverty, but his life was also inestimably enriched and guided by "prayer, longing, and faith," so we can thus discern how important this work of becoming "inwardly recollected" is for an evangelizer. In this connection, we can locate this cultivation of interior docility on an image of evangelization given by John Paul II, who distinguishes between evangelization *ad extra* and *ad intra*. In *Redemptoris Missio*, John Paul II argues that evangelization is not limited to those outside, or on the periphery, of the flock, but involves the strengthening and formation of all the people of God in faith. Evangelization thus includes dimensions of ecclesial life interior to the Church, namely, activities like catechesis and formation. He distinguishes these two foci of evangelization in the language used by theologians to describe, on the one hand, the processions of the Divine Persons in the Trinity, with exteriorly focused evangelization being *ad extra*, meaning "to the outside," as with the procession of Christ as the incarnate Jesus of Nazareth or the descent of the Holy Spirit at Pentecost. On the other hand, he calls evangelization focused within the Church as catechesis and formation *ad intra*, or "to the inside," which is traditionally assigned to the procession of the Divine Persons from all eternity "before the womb of the dawn" in the infinite blessedness of the divine life. Arrupe's writings on prayer in relation to inculturation offer the deepest (and most interior) dimensions of *ad intra* evangelization—not only proclaiming Christ and his Church to believers, but being addressed ("evangelized") by God himself in the solitude of one's own intimate personhood.

Moreover, Arrupe's tireless devotion to others stands in a long tradition of "living for others" displayed by Catholic witnesses throughout the ages. In this connection, it is worthwhile calling to mind a phrase used by Pope Francis (himself a Jesuit who served under Arrupe's leadership) in *Evangelii Gaudium*. There, the Holy Father reminds us that "evangelizers…take on the 'smell of the sheep' and the sheep are willing to hear their voice" (§24). This phrase is suggestive not merely of living among the people one feels called to evangelize, but immersing oneself in their communities, thoroughly understanding the perspective of those formed by their culture—being able to see the world with their eyes. This is not entirely dissimilar to certain approaches taken by anthropologists and ethnographers, who live among the people they are studying to imbue themselves deeply with their distinctive humanity. This has been discussed by the cultural commentator Susan Sontag, who argues that it is surely no accident that anthropology as an academic discipline arose after the Industrial Revolution and the acceleration of modernity in the West, developments that caused many to feel that traditional modes of social organization had been uprooted, creating a neuralgic sense of "homelessness." Sontag highlights the "inhuman acceleration of historical change" that "has led every sensitive modern mind to the recording of some kind of nausea."[13] In this sense, the fieldwork of cultural anthropologists involves something like "taking on the smell of the sheep," or what Sontag calls cultivating a "profoundly intelligent sympathy" with societies very different from one's own.[14] The basic point here is that, in tilling the soil, one must also cultivate this "profoundly intelligent sympathy" for those one seeks to evangelize; one must "take on the smell of the sheep."

Considered in this way, we can understand Arrupe's words: "If we want ourselves to be caught up in the process of inculturation, theory and study are not enough. We need the 'shock' of a deep personal experience." He then states that "for those called to live in another culture, it will mean being integrated in a new country, a new language, a whole new life. For those who remain in their own country, it will mean experiencing the new styles of our changing contemporary world—not the mere theoretical knowledge of the new mentalities, but the experiential assimilation of the way of life of the groups with which we must work, the outcasts, Chicanos, slum dwellers, intellectuals, students, artists, etc." Taking on the smell of sheep is thus called "total inculturation" by Arrupe.[15]

Although in terms of "method" or "approach" there are some similarities between cultural anthropology and "taking on the smell of the sheep," evangelization and anthropological research obviously differ deeply in their character and ends. The latter is clearly an attempt at *enculturation*, the process by which someone encountering a new culture undergoes "the process of socialization into that new culture."[16] We have seen this differs from *inculturation* primarily because, in becoming enculturated, one is not seeking to develop or transform the culture in question. However, Susan Sontag makes an interesting point about cultural anthropologists that offers further relevance to our examination of Arrupe, for she highlights that there is a certain paradox inherent in the immersion in a host culture by cultural anthropologists. Although anthropologists immerse themselves in a host culture and become enculturated to it, Sontag points out that they also garner things to take back to their own university cultures (invariably Western), where they unthinkingly accept what she calls "the philistine formulas of modern scientific 'value neutrality.'"[17] With this phrase, Sontag is arguing that, while anthropological interlopers fully accept the terms (values) of the culture they are studying, surrendering themselves to it in radical openness, they then expose these cultures to systematic intellectual study, which presupposes that modern academic study is entirely transcendent to culture—or exhibits "value neutrality." There is a paradox, here, for if one genuinely takes on the smell of the sheep, surely one's own value system must be altered, and surely nothing can be set apart as transcendent *to* culture. Sontag presents the bifurcation of practicing cultural immersion while holding that a scientific study is transcendent to culture as something almost schizophrenic in its inconsistency.

Issues with Inculturation

Inculturation clearly has certain strengths as previously outlined, and serves as a fruitful outworking of certain aspects of *Gaudium et Spes*, namely, the optimistic definition of *culture* and the praise of the emergent universality of modernity. But reflecting on Sontag's discussion of cultural anthropology leads us to ask if there are parallel problems in Arrupe. That is, we might ask if Arrupe is guilty of presupposing a certain neutrality to the gospel by holding that it can be incarnated in any host setting, if Christ is stripped of his concreteness and made a vacuous archetype, a characterless "universal human" and not the living embodied person that he is. In examining this question, we must keep in mind the resources provided by the previous chapter, the exhortation that "the Church's objective is to evangelize, not to civilize," and the distinction between a "better [*meliorum*] world" and the "new" world of the gospel. Let us, therefore, evaluate inculturation with the conditions on evangelizing as tilling the soil previously outlined, asking the following: Does it threaten mistakenly to appropriate the mission of the Church as a mission to civilize (cultivate values), and thereby stand in danger of confusing the distinction between a "better" and a "new" world? In answering these questions, the worth of bringing Mary as the Mirror of Justice into dialogue with inculturation will emerge.

First, criticisms can be put to Arrupe in that his reading of *Gaudium et Spes* seems to dissolve the tension the previous chapter sought to adhere to, which is important for the overall analysis of this book. Put simply, he rests entirely on the optimistic definition of *culture* as inherently edifying, and seems to sidestep the "difficulties" outlined in article 56. With this approach, all cultures are essentially constructive and formative of human personhood, and culture *of itself* nourishes human values and brings them to fruition. The problems with this have been highlighted already, for it is not difficult to find cultural expressions that seem devoid of redeeming features, most obviously in the state-sponsored art of Nazi Germany, but also much closer to home, for example, in the sadomasochistic paintings of Francis Bacon. Cultural expressions like these lead us to question whether culture itself is always intrinsically edifying, or sometimes ambivalent and able to work for either good or ill. This question does not seem to come onto Arrupe's horizon explicitly, for he makes no clear distinction between constructive and destructive cultural expressions, and seems to presuppose that all cultures are essentially of equal value. Here, we see that Sontag's reservations about cultural anthropology are mirrored in Arrupe, for there is a certain "neutrality" at work in the latter too.

One might defend Arrupe, here, by pointing out that his "mission field" was Japan and South America, and he was dealing with ancient cultures of some nobility, not the "modern culture" on which *Gaudium et Spes* is focused. This could mean the ambivalence of culture was less of an issue for him, as he was not dealing with the arguably more problematic realm of modern culture, characterized, as Sontag tells us, by the "inhuman acceleration of historical change" leading to "nausea" and "homelessness." But things are not quite so clear cut, for first, Arrupe draws on the description of modern culture in this conciliar text that praises the emergent universality of modernity, as we have seen. Second, moreover, he explicitly mentions the modern cultures of the West when he—with impressive foresight—touches upon issues that would now be classed as pertaining to the *New* Evangelization. He is thus speaking not only of "pre-Christian" or "non-Christian" contexts, like Japan in the early twentieth century, but of the cultures of nations that are "post-Christian" and have neglected or dismissed their Christian heritage. He writes that "today there is need of a new and continuous inculturation of the faith everywhere if we want the Gospel message to reach modern man" and that it "would be a dangerous error to deny that these areas need a *re-inculturation* of the faith."[18] In this connection, we might ask if post-Christian cultures are also called "to form, with mutual enrichment and complementarity, the 'robe of many colors' of the cultural reality of the one pilgrim People of God"?[19] Arrupe claims that "inculturation is the incarnation of Christian life and of the Christian message in a particular cultural context, in such a way that this experience…finds expression through elements proper to the culture in question." So, what happens if there are no, or very few, elements of a culture that can incarnate Christ in this thoroughgoing way?

With his optimistic approach to culture, we might well ask what Arrupe envisages when he states that the "Christian experience in a given culture has an influence that transforms and renews and, perhaps, after a *crisis of confrontation*, leads to a fresh wholeness in that culture."[20] That is, the omission of discussing the ambivalence of culture in *Gaudium et Spes* hinders us from ascertaining why there needs to be a crisis of confrontation. Moreover, in Arrupe's reference to the Spiritual Exercises, the Word is incarnated to diverse peoples who are hardly affirmed in and of themselves, but are actually going to hell, for the retreatant is commended to "hear what the persons on the face of the earth are saying—the way they talk to each other and how they swear and blaspheme, etc."[21] So, the question arises here of whether there is a more ambivalent attitude to culture at work in Arrupe, for surely there could be cultural analogues to the seething and blaspheming mass of humanity visualized by St. Ignatius.

What inculturation seems to require, therefore, is a means to discern the worth of diverse cultural expressions, something to ensure not all cultures are simply understood as being intrinsically edifying. Drawing on one of our key moments from *Gaudium et Spes*, genuinely edifying culture will be that which builds up "a better world in truth and justice." We will focus on truth in the following chapter; however, considering that justice is central for Arrupe, let us examine briefly this concept. Arrupe speaks of the "Gospel of love," but argues that "love demands justice" and he therefore speaks also of the "Gospel of justice." In his writing on the "social apostolate" of the Jesuits, he makes justice central, arguing for a "just order based on equity." He states elsewhere, moreover, that "education for justice has become…one of the chief concerns of the Church" because "promotion of justice" is, in fact, "a constitutive element of the mission which Our Lord has entrusted to her."[22] What we would expect to see when evangelizing through inculturation, therefore, is a seeking for the value of *justice* in a host culture, as something right and proper that will find its ultimate fulfillment in Christ.

Justice is also prevalent in contemporary culture as a key value in the self-understanding of modernity. Arrupe's words about seeking a "just order based on equity" would thus find many sympathetic ears outside the religious sphere today. This is shown paradigmatically in the Universal Declaration of Human Rights, which starts by asserting that "the inherent dignity" and "the equal and inalienable rights of all members of the human family is the foundation of freedom, justice and peace in the world," and goes on to expound the various ramifications of the conviction that "all human beings are born free and equal in dignity and rights." Presupposing that "all human beings are born free and equal," the Declaration commends that all are entitled to a certain level of respect. Perhaps surprisingly, this declaration (and therefore the ethical norms of the modern world) is at least partly rooted in classical culture. In ancient Greece and Rome, there are numerous examples of the principle *suum cuique*, meaning "the notion that each man is to be given his due."[23] It is a basic principle for human sociality, found as early as Homer's *Odyssey*, Plato's *Republic*, and in Aristotle and Cicero. Through this lineage in the Western tradition, it passed into the tradition of the Church, being found in Ambrose and Augustine, and maintained today as a "cardinal virtue" in the modern-day *Catechism*, drawing on Aquinas's view that justice (or *iustitia*), is "a habit, whereby a man renders to each one his due with constant and perpetual will."[24]

So justice is central for Arrupe, and for our world today, while being rooted in classical culture and passing therefrom into the tradition of the Church. It is, however, also a deeply scriptural term, for the Latin word *iustitia* was used in the Vulgate and Old Latin translations of the Scriptures to translate the original term δικαιοσύνη (*dikaiosynē*), which is now usually translated as "righteousness" in English. In basic terms, to be "righteous" in the worldview of Holy Scripture means to be conformed to God's will, to participate in his life through a worldly existence of obedience and prayer. This is how we can understand the Beatitude "blessed are those who hunger and thirst for righteousness" (Matt 5:6); Jesus's statement that the Holy Spirit "will prove the world wrong about sin and righteousness" (John 16:8); Peter's words about doing "what is right" (Acts 10:35); or the words of the Canticle of Zechariah, which speak of serving the Lord "in holiness and righteousness" (Luke 1:75). It is, however, also clear in the Scriptures that righteousness is not a mere human quality but also about participating in God himself. That is, to be "righteous" or serving God "in righteousness" is to be caught up in the divine life; righteousness thus somehow originates in God. This can be seen when Jesus speaks of serving "*his* righteousness" (Matt 6:33), or James's discussion of "God's righteousness" (Jas 1:20), and at numerous points in Paul's letters, particularly Romans, where he speaks at length about "the righteousness of God" (e.g., Rom 1:17; 3:5, 21–26). Paul is, of course, drawing deeply on righteousness as understood in the Hebrew Scriptures, as *sedeq* was translated using δικαιοσύνη (*dikaiosynē*) in the Septuagint. In the Old Testament, someone is righteous through being faithful to the covenant promises made with God, but again, God himself is also righteous on account of his covenantal faithfulness. Righteousness in the Old Testament thus means God honors his promises—he holds to the pledges made with integrity and in love, and not "in terms of 'right' or ethical conduct as determined by some abstract standard."[25] In short, *righteousness* is a relational, participatory term, intrinsically and unavoidably linked with God's *person*, and not, therefore, merely a principle of good conduct in and of itself.

The foregoing discussion suggests some dissonance between classical notions of justice as *suum cuique*, or Arrupe's "just order based on equity," and scriptural righteousness as something concretely personal and relational. However, there is, here, a further layer of complexity, in that analogues to the classical understanding of *iustitia* passed into the Scriptures themselves as well. This is to be expected, for many scriptural authors shared times and places with elements of classical culture, and after all, "words neither exist by themselves without a context, nor are texts written as free-floating packages of meaning without…a place in their historical milieu."[26] This is demonstrated by Peter's words of encouragement to the pagan family of Cornelius that "in every nation anyone who fears him and does what is right is acceptable to [God]" (Acts 10:35), or Titus's description of a righteous person (Titus 1:8), or the prophet Micah's commendation for the people of Israel to "do justice" (Mic 6:8), or even in the understanding of giving what each one deserves in the Pentateuch and Isaiah (cf. Deut 25:1; Exod 23:7; Isa 50:8).

So, if we are to take justice as a means of evaluating a cultural setting within inculturation, and must look for justice as our point of contact or resonance from which to embark on our proclamation of the gospel of Christ, we find two broad approaches to justice in Scripture and Tradition. There is, first, the basic principle or value of human nature, *suum cuique*, and second, the personal and participatory life in the justice of God himself. Taking the *suum cuique* first, we have seen this aligns with Arrupe's words about "a just order based on equity." Here, something surprising comes to light, as for all Arrupe's commendations of the apparently equal worth of cultures, he is himself unavoidably formed by classical culture, perhaps by being Catholic, or maybe simply as a Westerner. This means there is a tension in Arrupe. On the one hand, he seems to envisage "Christian life and the Christian message" as able to speak in any cultural context, and therefore to be transcendent to culture, like the oneness he spoke of amongst the Jesuits at the Thirty-Second

General Congregation, the "overwhelming consciousness of belonging together." He thus presents inculturation as involving an understanding of Christian life rather like a tasteless, colorless, and invisible form of living without concrete attributes, which can enter any circumstances and vivify them with the light of Christ. However, if we try to pinpoint completely extracultural aspects of Christian life, we have a challenging task ahead of us, and this is true of Arrupe's own work.

On this point, Arrupe's consideration of culture as inherently edifying—his one-sided reading of *Gaudium et Spes*—presents a further issue. Arrupe seems not only to consider any cultural setting as able to bring Christ to birth on its own terms, but even to consider Christ, himself, as somehow present latently in human culture in and of itself. This is shown by his claim that "seeds of the Word" (*semina Verbi*) are present in host cultures, and are something an evangelizer must seek out. He argues that "inculturation requires a *persevering patience*," for "it is necessary patiently to search for the *semina Verbi*," which are "predestined by Providence for the building up of truth."[27] This is a strong claim, for language of *semina Verbi* takes us away from evangelizing as tilling the soil, in that by seeking for seeds of the Word one is not preparing the ground *for* Christ as such, because Christ is understood to be already present, as dormant, in a host culture. For this reason, searching for *semina Verbi* is not sowing the seed either, for it presupposes the seed is *already* sown.

So, speaking of *semina Verbi* threatens to make the proclamation of, or the witness to, Christ superfluous, for Christ is already "there," lying dormant in the worldview of an addressee. The problem, here, is that it threatens to contradict the key conditions of tilling the soil provided for us by *Gaudium et Spes*. If Christ is already present latently in a host culture and brought to fruition by the cultivation of value, then the Church's mission stands in real danger of being mistakenly appropriated as a mission to civilize: a mission to cultivate values as an end in itself. Moreover, if Christ is latent within culture and brought to birth by the cultivation of value, then cultivating value is in real danger of being understood as something that can bring not just a better world, but the genuinely *novum* world redeemed by Christ.

We thus find a distinction between approaching a cultural setting as ground that can be prepared for evangelization by tilling the soil, and the stronger claim that cultural settings contain *semina Verbi*. If we are to keep to the creative tension of *Gaudium et Spes*, then, tilling the soil must be approached only as preparing the ground for the gospel, and not as a seeking after *semina Verbi*. Speaking of a preparation for the gospel, of course, has its own nomenclature in the Catholic tradition: *praeparatio evangelica*. This term *praeparatio evangelica* stems from the early apologists and Church fathers, who considered their specific cultural context at that point in history as a *praeparatio evangelica*. This brings us back to classical thought again. This point is borne out by the fact that certain elements of classical thinking have made their way into authoritative formulations of Catholic doctrine, most famously in the Greek philosophical terminology of being (*ousia*), person (*hypostasis*), and consubstantiality in the formulations of the doctrines of the Trinity at Nicaea-Constantinople, and the incarnation at Chalcedon. More substantially, we also find that some classical thinking centered on an approach to reason as logos that could align, to a considerable degree, with the Logos of John's Gospel, the light of reason that lights up everyone who enters the world.

Now, we can bring these more negative evaluations of Arrupe to a close with two findings, which, as we will note, arise from considering the Blessed Virgin as the Mirror of Justice, showing that Mary as the Star of Evangelization serves as a corrective to problematic or misconstrued approaches to evangelization, and thereby the formative power of Marian piety. First, by cultivating a response in the addressees of evangelization through tilling the soil, the gospel cannot rightly be transcendent to culture, but is unavoidably intertwined with classical culture. Second, tilling the soil must be approached only as *reflecting* the light of Christ, and care must be taken to ensure that the mere cultivation of values is not mistakenly confused with Christ's person in and of itself.

MARY AS MIRROR OF JUSTICE

In conclusion, the pressures bearing on evangelizing as tilling the soil through inculturation can be suitably adhered to if we approach it as the "mirroring of justice." First, although inculturation certainly has strengths in its highlighting of interiority and "taking on the smell of the sheep," it also has the danger of seeing the gospel as completely transcendent to culture. The foregoing investigation has shown that—regarding justice—the Scriptures, and even Arrupe himself, are unavoidably formed by the cultural background of the classical world, namely the *suum cuique*. For this reason, for inculturation to proceed as genuine evangelization, the cultivation of values should be configured by the distinctive cultural heritage of the Catholic tradition. This means that not all values are nurtured by tilling the soil, and that some settings might prove inimical to the proclamation, but also that an inculturator can cultivate values insofar as those values genuinely mirror those of Scripture and Tradition. This case was made earlier with the paradigmatic value of justice or righteousness, and thus we saw that inculturation, in line with the conditions laid out in *Gaudium et Spes*, must be a mirroring of *justice*, reflecting genuine *righteousness* as found in Catholic teaching. This means that the Church's mission stays focused on evangelization, and is not mistaken as a mission to civilize. Yet, insofar as right civic conduct is found in the tradition, with the *suum cuique*, the Church may civilize by evangelizing. Or rather, "the Church, *in the very fulfillment of her own function*, stimulates and advances human and civic culture; by her action" (*Gaudium et Spes* 58).[28]

Second, Arrupe's description of inculturation considers Christ to be present in any cultural setting as *semina Verbi*. Our discussion has shown that this threatens to make evangelization unnecessary, for simply by cultivating the values of a culture one might seem to be incarnating Christ himself. For this reason, inculturation should proceed under the condition that it is only tilling the soil by cultivating values, and that the proclamation of Christ himself necessitates *sowing* the seed. So, again, inculturation must be approached as a *mirroring*, a reflecting of Christ in the light of cultures, and not as directly bringing Christ to bear in that culture itself. In this sense, the cultivation of value by evangelization is sharply distinguished from cultivating values in and of themselves. Evangelization is not only then understood as a means to make the world more just (or "better"), but as a means for Christ be born anew in the world, inaugurating in a world in which all things are "made new" (cf. Rev 21:5).

These two findings emphasize the point made in the introduction, where the hidden depths of Mary as Star of Evangelization can be brought into view. Inculturation must be a mirroring of justice, an ancient title of Our Lady. Our evangelizing through inculturation should therefore proceed through conformation to the figure of Mary, in whom is found the perfect response to the call of faith, the one who is hallowed by tradition to be the "good soil," the *terra immaculata*. In seeking to understand Mary's ancient title of Mirror of Justice more deeply, we should discern her deep interrelatedness with righteousness as described by Scripture. That she is personally just and righteousness is of course well attested by tradition as far back as *Protoevangelium of James* (ca. AD 145),[29] and that she intimately participates in God's divine life is aptly demonstrated in Luke's Gospel (cf. 1:38; 2:51). But, we even find traces of justice or righteousness as the *suum cuique* connected with Mary, not least in the Magnificat, which states that God has filled the hungry with good things (Luke 1:53). If we evangelize by inculturation, in accordance with the conditions of *Gaudium et Spes*, we are faced with something distinctively Marian: we are called to be mirrors of *justice*, construed as mirroring the righteousness of God, as well as the *suum cuique*, that is, in a way, already configured in part by the cultural influence of the classical world.

Moreover, we are called to *mirror* justice, to hold before us a firm distinction between tilling the soil and sowing the seed. In this sense, the depth of Mary's ancient image of being a mirror can be seen. This is connected to the plethora of lunar imagery in Marian iconography, drawing on her reflecting the light of Christ as the moon reflects the sun, or Christ as the "sun of righteousness" (Mal 4:2). Consequently, there is a firm distinction between tilling the soil and sowing the seed, for to prepare the ground for Christ, to till the soil, is not to claim that Christ himself is lying dormant in a host culture, but to seek to mirror him. In this, the sowing of the seed itself is maintained as something different: something that can make "all things new." Such are the formative and corrective impulses inherent in devotion to Mary as the Mirror of Justice, arising from considering justice as a criterion for interpreting the value of different cultural settings. To point to the following chapter, let us remember that *Gaudium et Spes* highlights two values as highly important in the world's development: "truth and justice." Having given considerable attention to justice, our focus in the next chapter will be on truth.

Chapter 3

Interculturality

Mary as "Seat of Wisdom"

THE PREVIOUS CHAPTER revealed some of the hidden depths of considering Mary as the Star of Evangelization. We discerned that evangelizing by tilling the soil through inculturation could present certain problems, but by conforming our activities to the figure of Mary through her title Mirror of Justice, we are aligned in a way that promises to ensure that we proceed in keeping with the creative tension of *Gaudium et Spes*. Inculturation involves, of course, the preparation of the ground for the gospel by cultivating the goods and values of human nature. As we saw in the introduction, this side of evangelization is expressed by Paul VI's "central axis" that makes the message as "understandable and persuasive as possible." With elements from a cultural setting that mirror scriptural justice and the light of Christ, the gospel message will be even more compelling and is thereby accommodated *to* its addressees.

In this chapter, we proceed from our discussion of Arrupe to focus on evangelizing by sowing the seed. Recall that this aligns with the other side to Paul VI's central axis, namely, preserving the "untouchable purity" of the message. Here, we move from seeking to fit the message to the worldview of its hearers, to seeking to ensure it is communicated genuinely and authentically. However, the previous chapter presents us with a complexity to sowing the seed not immediately apparent before examining Arrupe. The seed of Catholic teaching already contains cultural elements: the proclamation is not transcendent to culture, for it already has elements of the classical culture of the ancient world weaved into it. This reconfigures our investigation, for it suggests that sowing the seed of Catholic teaching involves the meeting of (at least) two cultural influences. There is, on the one hand, the content of evangelization, which is intertwined with classical culture, and on the other, the host culture being evangelized. Now, the resplendence of Christ refracting outward by holding the two sides to *Gaudium et Spes* in tension brings forth a new and different beam of light. This new beam points away from inculturation and may bring us nearer to *acculturation*, the contact between two cultures in which both are transformed, with deep-rooted changes resulting in each. Catholic teaching, however, is, of course, more than a mere culture, so one would not expect sowing the seed to result in arbitrary changes and adaptations to Catholic life. This means that, in the contact between Catholic teaching and a host culture that takes place in sowing the seed, there needs to be a basis for their mutual transformation, a grounding rationale or evaluative criterion that defines and determines how they can interpenetrate, to maintain the "untouchable purity" of the message itself.

To understand this second beam of light, we will examine the theology of culture of Joseph Ratzinger, connected with the term *interculturality*. In this, we encounter a grounding rationale that promises to provide the grounding basis required, namely *truth*. Ratzinger's work demonstrates that, insofar as a culture has engendered or cultivated that which is true, it will organically intertwine with Catholic teaching, for he considers Catholic teaching to be grounded on the God who is "Truth itself" (*Catechism* 215).[1] For Ratzinger, an encounter between two true "things" cannot contradict each other; what is true will inevitably intertwine with the gospel and not confront it destructively. However, notwithstanding the benefits of sowing the seed based on truth, there is a possible drawback regarding this emphasis. A focus on truth can lead to a one-size-fits-all understanding of reality, which is not mindful enough of cultural difference and specificity, nor the slow maturation of worldviews over vast expanses of time. Indeed, we saw an analogous point acknowledged in *Gaudium et Spes*, which asks, "What is to be done to prevent...disturbing the life of communities, from destroying the wisdom received from ancestors, or from placing in danger the character proper to each people?" (§56). The conciliar fathers respond to this by modifying the focus on sheer truth to thinking instead in terms of wisdom, which maintains a sense of the rightness and accuracy of the true, with a sensitivity toward cultural difference and temporal development.

Ratzinger thus offers us a grounding basis for sowing the seed, and *Gaudium et Spes* directs us toward understanding this basis in terms not only of truth, but of wisdom. Once again, the depths of Mary as Star of Evangelization emerge, here, through another title of the Litany of Loreto: "Seat of Wisdom." Insofar as truth offers a grounding basis for sowing the seed, we can consider it as a "seat," a resting place, or a locus of support for the work of evangelization. Insofar as we approach the truth of sowing the seed as wisdom, we find that, based on their truth, different worldviews can intertwine with Catholic teaching in the development of wisdom. Sowing the seed through interculturality, therefore, finds its exemplary focal point and paradigm in Mary as the Seat of Wisdom.

JOSEPH RATZINGER

Joseph Ratzinger needs little introduction for the obvious reason that he became Pope Benedict XVI in 2005, and held an eight-year pontificate. Consequently, we will briefly outline some aspects of his papacy relevant to this book, and then study two speeches made prior to his enthronement, in which he engages in a critical dialogue with inculturation and enunciates an alternative approach. First, it has been suggested the papal name, Benedict, was taken partly in homage to St. Benedict, the patron saint of Europe.[2] Benedict XVI was deeply concerned about the Christian heritage of Europe at a time of increasing secularization and several types of "de-Christianization." This concern, of course, relates to this book, insofar as it led Benedict XVI to reflect deeply on the interrelation of faith and culture. He thus spoke often on the history of the European and American continents, and examined how these relate to the history of the Church in other settings. Directly related to this is the second pertinent theme of his papacy: the New Evangelization. Benedict XVI founded the Pontifical Council for Promoting the New Evangelization in 2010, and regularly indicated his desire to see the secularized and allegedly "post-Christian" cultures of the Western world evangelized afresh by the gospel of Christ and his Church.

Joseph Ratzinger published a vast number of books and articles. However, the following discussion focuses on two writings that are particularly pertinent for us. The first is his address "Christ, Faith and the Challenge of Cultures" given in Hong Kong to the presidents of the Asian bishops' conferences in 1993. In this address, Ratzinger argues that the term *inculturation* should no longer be used, and that it should be replaced with a new term, our theme for this chapter: *interculturality*.[3] Inculturation had been a major concern of the Asian bishops for some years, not least because of the experience of Christian evangelization in the Indian subcontinent. There, the level of cultural diversity was so immense, and the religious plurality so broad, that the work of evangelization was extremely complex and led to much discussion about the dynamics of proclaiming Christ in cultures radically different from those where Christianity was historically established. Many of these discussions touch upon our own, as they involve the degree to which the proclamation of Christ should be adjusted to be made as understandable and persuasive as possible, while still maintaining the faith in untouchable purity to retain its integrity. As we will see, Ratzinger addressed the Asian bishops' conferences with a perspective that resonates strongly with the findings of the last chapter: inculturation presents certain problems, particularly in the degree to which it can be expected to maintain the faith in its untouchable purity, that is, when it is applied to sowing the seed.

Here, we will also draw on a second address given some six years later, at St. Patrick's Seminary in the Archdiocese of San Francisco. In this address, Ratzinger reflects on John Paul II's encyclical *Fides et Ratio*, which had been promulgated six months previously. In this document, John Paul II states, "In engaging great cultures for the first time, the Church cannot abandon what she has gained from her inculturation in the world of Greco-Latin thought. To reject this heritage would be to deny the providential plan of God who guides his Church down the paths of time and history" (§72). This sentiment challenges some of Pedro Arrupe's presuppositions, for he does not make any one culture intrinsically related to the proclamation of the Church over against any others, and holds all cultures as equally valuable, each containing the *semina Verbi* within them. It should be apparent that, given Benedict XVI's concern for the Christian heritage of Europe, he would want to explore this point of disagreement between *Fides et Ratio* and Arrupe, and indeed this is certainly perceptible in the texts examined here. We can thus discern that Ratzinger's starting point in these addresses is roughly aligned with our own: seeking to evangelize by sowing the seed as a meeting of cultures while maintaining the "untouchable purity" of the message.

INTERCULTURALITY

A Basis for the Meeting of Cultures

As mentioned at the outset, if we acknowledge that Catholic teaching involves cultural elements and is not transcendent to culture, how are we to keep "sowing the seed" from leading to acculturation, the haphazard intertwining of two distinct cultures? Ratzinger sketches an answer to this question, not merely through discussing culture in relation to Christian life, but by focusing on culture itself, which had been given a great deal of attention by the intellectual tradition of his German homeland. In "Christ, Faith, and the Challenge of Cultures," Ratzinger makes suggestions for defining culture in and of itself, so that for him, culture and religion are deeply and inextricably interrelated. This enables us to build on the finding of the previous chapter that the gospel is not transcendent to culture, for Ratzinger concludes that all religious expressions must be, to some degree, cultural. He argues that "in all known historical cultures, religion is the essential element of culture, indeed it is its determining core." His reason for taking this bold stance, is that "it is religion which determines the structure of values and thereby forms [a culture's] inner logic."[4] He thus implies that cultures always include values, and, in reality, there is no culture that is not fundamentally based on religion. At this point, you would be forgiven for asking about explicitly atheistic cultural expressions like those previously mentioned, coming from the Soviet Union and parts of the secularized West. However, Ratzinger's analysis suggests that such examples are not genuinely "historical," meaning not having a long pedigree matured over great distances of time, and growing organically in the soil of a certain people. Explicitly atheistic cultures are not only of recent provenance, but, in cases like Soviet Communism, they are not the product of organic development but rather of deliberate and conscious ideological imposition.

Ratzinger's view that culture and religion are always inextricably intertwined works from his view of culture as "an attempt to understand the world and man's existence in the world," which "should show us how to be human, how man is to take his proper place in this world and respond to it in order to realize himself in his search for success and happiness." This means that culture always "encompasses the indispensable dimension of values or morals" and "always contains the prior and actually foundational question of God."[5] In short, culture cannot be separated from values, from principled convictions about what is *good* and *true* and therefore worthwhile. Moreover, looking at a broad sweep of human history over the millennia, there are no systems of value that are not rooted in some form of religion and thereby contain this "prior question" of God. That is, if cultures delineate the structures of being properly human in the world, they are enmeshed with means of evaluating that which is proper and good, and evaluations of the good are invariably interrelated with some sense of an ultimate or highest good, most commonly understood to be God.

Nonetheless, for the contemporary West, this intertwining of religion and culture might seem a little out of step with the popular mindset, and Ratzinger discusses why this is. He asserts that the idea of separating religion and culture is essentially a product of the Enlightenment. He thus argues that only in "modern Europe," that is, post-Enlightenment Europe, a concept of culture has originated holding that culture has "its own domain distinct from, or even in opposition to, religion."[6] For Ratzinger the notion of an autonomously human culture stripped of a religious grounding is an invention of Western modernity. He states clearly that the very idea of culture ever being without religion is a modern innovation with no ancient pedigree. This leads us to an interesting implication: the theory of inculturation, by assuming that the gospel is transcendent to culture, is to some extent inadvertently marked by the Enlightenment. This might lead some to question its authenticity as genuinely rooted in ancient Christian tradition in the form with which Arrupe presents it. This would certainly seem to hold for Ratzinger. Because Ratzinger considers culture and religion always to be inextricably intertwined, he critiques inculturation on the same grounds as the previous chapter, since Catholic teaching is inevitably already cultural. He argues that inculturation "presumes that a faith stripped of culture is transplanted into a religiously indifferent culture whereby two subjects, formerly unknown to each other, meet and fuse." The reality is quite different, for, as he puts it, "there is no such thing as a faith devoid of culture or culture devoid of faith."[7]

We have already discerned that Catholic faith is not devoid of culture, but with Ratzinger's assertion that no culture is devoid of faith either, we can appreciate how this must affect a strategy of evangelization. From the perspective of this theology of culture, when sowing the seed of Catholic teaching, one need not only assess how amicable that context may or may not be to the message of Christ and his Church, but also be sensitive to the distinctly *religious* parameters of that cultural setting. These may not be explicit, but could manifest as systems of value, or an orientation to a conceived form of highest good, or transcendence. The questions an evangelizer must ask are, "What does this culture value the most?" or "What does this culture presuppose about the ultimate destiny of human beings?" and so on.

In being sensitive to the religious elements of a host culture, one must, of course, have equal sensitivity to the cultural elements of one's own faith. Regarding Catholic teaching, we have seen that ancient classical culture is particularly important, as recognized by *Fides et Ratio*. Taking this point on board and incorporating it into a strategy of evangelization, questions such as those just formulated would involve not merely asking questions about ultimate values and ends in the worldview of addresses of the proclamation in relation to the gospel, but also being aware of the cultural heritage attached to the message of the gospel, through the Scriptures themselves and Tradition. We saw this interconnectedness in the last chapter, through discerning that when seeking "mirrors of justice" in a host culture, the sense of justice involved must have some resonance with justice as construed by classical culture, that is, the *suum cuique*. But this leaves us with a difficult challenge. When evangelizing, we are doing more than simply bringing two cultures into relation to each other; we are not undertaking a mere cultural fusion, like acculturation. This means that the claims of the gospel cannot simply be adjusted to another culture in a haphazard or arbitrary way, without undermining their authenticity. If we, following Ratzinger, accept that Catholic teaching is always already cultural, and a host culture is to some extent always already religious (or at least involves some religious or pseudoreligious presuppositions), we thus need some basis for evangelization, a rationale that will enable an evangelizer to establish the grounds on which the meeting and fusing of two sets of cultural elements should proceed without inadvertently neglecting, neutralizing, or even negating the gospel itself. In short, we need to understand how we might go about sowing the seed in untouchable purity.

Ratzinger provides us with an answer to this question himself, which arises from his distinctive understanding of the nobility and greatness of classical culture. For him, there is a certain character to Greco-Latin cultural expression that is a paradigmatic or exemplary instance of a process at work in many cultures, particularly those of ancient pedigree. To bring this distinctive character into view, the first point to note is that Ratzinger highlights the *universalism* of classical thought. In other words, the reason for classical culture functioning as a preparation of the ground for the taking root of the gospel is that it cultivated certain convictions. To give a basic example of this, we can cite what is perhaps the most fundamental conviction of classical culture in relation to the Christian dispensation: the understanding that all human beings belong to one universal human species. This seems so obvious to us today that it is easy to underestimate its importance. But, prior to the development of classical culture, many historians and philosophers consider that worldviews were largely limited to only one set of people, one ethnicity or group of ethnicities. In the classical world, the conviction became explicit and central that there is such a thing as human *nature*, a broad set of characteristics pertaining to all people by definition, a nature that is universally human. This is closely related to the classical understanding of "reason" or *logos*: the view that human beings are universally endowed with a faculty of reason, something pertaining to all people by virtue of their humanity, a necessary feature of human nature. Because classical culture ascertained that there is a universal human nature, seen particularly in the universal endowment of reason, the proclamation that Jesus Christ is the Savior of *all* people (cf. John 12:32; 1 Tim 4:10), in fact, the very *Logos* of God himself, found fertile soil that made that proclamation genuinely compelling in a way that would not otherwise have been possible.

This understanding of classical culture as *praeparatio evangelica* based on its universalism is widespread in Catholic theology. Ratzinger discusses this at length, working from the view that "only if all cultures are potentially universal and open to each other" can the intermingling with new, external elements—such as happens in evangelization—"lead to flourishing new forms." He then goes on to ask what this potential universality and openness found in cultures capable of this intermingling involves. He answers, first, by highlighting universality, arguing that the "the meeting of cultures is possible because man, despite all the differences of his history and social constructs, remains one and the same being."[8] He thus holds that cultures can only "meet and fuse" if they presuppose that all human beings share a universal nature. The most obvious example of a worldview questioning this conviction in modernity is Nazism, which considered so-called non-Aryan persons "sub-human" (*untermenschlich*). It is worth remembering, here, that some of Ratzinger's childhood overlapped with the Third Reich, so he saw the appallingly destructive effects of this barbaric attempt at superiority firsthand. It should also be borne in mind that the undermining of human universality can be more subtle, as is seen in some examples of European imperialism in the nineteenth century that considered indigenous peoples less human than their conquerors. We even see universality undermined today in what is termed "cultural imperialism," the supposition that a certain way of doing things is inherently superior to others, to the degree that those who do not subscribe to it are somehow less than human.

But Ratzinger takes us deeper in his distinctive focus on universality, and in doing so, he sketches an answer for us to the question of how the meeting and fusing of two cultures should proceed in evangelization without lapsing into mere acculturation—how the proclamation of the gospel can be maintained in its untouchable purity. He does this by stating that "this one being man," that is, universal human nature, "is touched in the depth of his existence by *truth*. The fundamental openness of each person to the other can only be explained by the hidden fact that our souls have been touched by truth; this explains the essential agreement which exists even between cultures most removed from each other."[9] What he means by this is that it is not so much rationality as a universal endowment that grounds the universality of human nature, but rather the effects *of* rationality: an ability to conceive and judge matters *truly*, that is, accurately and in their fullness. Reason is thus something that enables people to discern universalities. On the most basic level, reason enables us to ascertain truths such as "every effect must have a cause," or that 12 x 12 = 144. Once such conclusions are arrived at in a rational, principled way, they must apply to all circumstances across time and space. They must pertain universally—there are no circumstances and no people to whom 12 x 12 can be anything other than 144. For Ratzinger, the key point is that human beings seek to understand the *truth* about themselves, the world in which they exist, and fundamental truths about existence, and, insofar as genuine truth is arrived at, it must be amicable to ultimate truth: truths about the God who is the source of existence and its final goal or telos.

So, Ratzinger holds that insofar as cultures are directed to attaining truth, or better, "touched by truth," they can transcend their own particularity.[10] This means that a culture that makes progress in discerning the truth of the human condition makes inroads into ways of thinking that bear on all people, not just those of that culture. A culture that ascertains something of the true reality of the world will uncover matters pertaining to all those who live in the world, and most importantly, a culture that has acquired some awareness of the ultimate truth undergirding all things can teach us something about the God from whence all things come. Perhaps this helps us to understand the incredible provenance of great cultural expressions that, while some might say they are not to their taste, undoubtedly exhibit a remarkable ability to take root in cultural settings vastly different from their origins. That is, perhaps the plays of Shakespeare disclose things that are universally true beyond sixteenth- and seventeenth-century England, or Bach's cantatas beyond seventeenth- and eighteenth- century Leipzig. Either way, Ratzinger concludes that cultures marked by truth exhibit what he terms "self-transcendence."[11] In other words, they rise above the limitations of their own people and circumstances, and encounter true realities pertaining to all people.

Joseph Ratzinger shows us that the discernment of the truth exhibited by classical culture is exemplary in its *self-transcendence*: in its ability to rise above the limited concerns of the ancient Mediterranean world, and uncover truths bearing on all human beings. He writes, "With the peoples of Asia, Africa and America, the Christian faith introduced these people not to Greek culture as such, but rather to its capacity for self-transcendence, which was the true connecting point for interpreting the Christian message."[12] He argues, therefore, that evangelization of these peoples "drew them into the dynamic of self-transcendence," and therefore, that when these peoples were introduced to classical thought through evangelization, "there was no intention to canonize a particular culture as such, but rather enter into it at the point where it had begun to transcend itself…to open itself to universal truth and thus to lead it out of the enclosure of pure particularity."[13]

This reconfigures our discussion considerably, for it provides us with an answer to the question of how evangelizing, while being mindful of the distinctive cultural patrimony of Catholic teaching, can avoid a haphazard or arbitrary cultural fusing. From Ratzinger's analysis we can discern that Catholic teaching—the proclamation of Christ and his Church—can intertwine and fuse with a host culture insofar as that culture encounters truth. True things cannot and will not contradict and challenge each other, and Ratzinger shows that truth can be discerned by humanity in and of itself, as exemplified by classical culture. In this sense, we need not assume that sowing the seed would be under threat of being injudiciously accommodated to the "webs of significance" of its addressees. Rather, insofar as these webs of significance are "touched by truth," they can be attuned to and weaved around Catholic teaching, and moreover, Catholic teaching itself can assimilate and interweave with forms of that host culture. So, the intermingling of cultures in evangelizing can take place based on truth, with their being "touched by" truth as the grounding rationale.

Moreover, Ratzinger's analysis shows that to proclaim Christ as "the truth" (John 14:6) will not contradict worldviews attuned to the truth. For Ratzinger, if a culture is capable of self-transcendence, then this capability is *by definition* an openness to Jesus Christ, for he maintains that "Christian faith is…certain that in its core it is the self-disclosure of truth itself."[14] That is, not only does the Christian proclamation disclose the definitive ultimate reality of humanity, the world, and God, but more extensively, Jesus Christ is the bringer of "grace and truth" (John 1:14, 17), the truth that "will make you free" (John 8:32), for God wants "everyone to be saved and to come to the knowledge of the truth" (1 Tim 2:4), and Jesus calls himself the "truth" (John 14:6). Jesus is the definitive revelation of God, the fullest and unsurpassable disclosure of God in and of himself. Moreover, the Holy Spirit, the active agent of evangelization, is the "Spirit of *truth*" (John 14:17). We would do well, here, to remember that the word for "truth" in the New Testament is ἀλήθεια (*alētheia*), which does not mean only that something corresponds to reality, in the sense of mirroring it, but that it *discloses* reality. In this sense, Jesus Christ is the definitive disclosure of ultimate truth.

In conclusion, let's examine exactly what Ratzinger's term *interculturality* means. He deliberately adopts this term as an alternative to *inculturation*,[15] criticizing inculturation as "artificial and unrealistic" for presuming that "a faith stripped of culture is transplanted into a religiously indifferent culture whereby two subjects, formerly unknown to each other, meet and fuse."[16] We can now appreciate that the *inter-* of interculturality refers to a thoroughgoing interchange or intercourse between two organisms, one of which has grown around the gospel, so that a "profound evolution" occurs by way of mutual interpenetration, which he terms a "successful transformation."[17] This is, therefore, not mere acculturation, for there is a grounding rationale by which it proceeds: the mutual encounter with truth, the encounter between Catholic teaching dispensed by the God who is truth itself, and the truths discerned by the host culture. Interculturality thus involves a fundamental basis of truth in evangelizing by sowing the seed, and this is the place where Catholic teaching can "rest" in a host culture, its place of support therein, is foundation.

In this connection, we now turn our attention to one of Mary's titles, Seat of Wisdom, which seems particularly apposite for sowing the seed through interculturality. That is, if acculturation is to be avoided, the fundamental basis is truth, and, in this sense, it can be considered a "seat"—the place of repose from which the seed can be sown and bear fruit proper to a host culture.

Truth and Wisdom

Before looking more deeply at Mary as a "seat" or place of repose in interculturality, let us conduct a more critical examination of interculturality through the lens of Mary's title Seat of Wisdom. Wisdom proved itself particularly important in our earlier discussion of *Gaudium et Spes*, where it functions as a corrective to the dangers of one side of the creative tension involved in culture. On the one hand, the positive, explicit definition of *culture* as that which edifies is said to have a positive outcome in fostering an awareness of universality in modern culture. The document thus states that "there develops a more universal form of human culture, which better promotes and expresses the unity of the human race to the degree that it preserves the particular aspects of the different civilizations" (§54). This aligns comfortably with Ratzinger's analysis, for as we have seen, Ratzinger considers that the *true* is the universal, what is true is true universally. The development of human technology and its effects on communication, and the growth of science, exhibit the human encounter with truth in modern culture and thereby foster a universality, a sense of oneness between peoples sharing a common destiny on earth.

However, *Gaudium et Spes* also sounds a note of caution about this newly emerging universalism. It asks, "What is to be done to prevent… disturbing the life of communities, from destroying the wisdom received from ancestors, or from placing in danger the character proper to each people?" (§56). We saw that this points to the fact that values of universality, fraternity, and mutual respect might threaten genuine diversity, drowning out the distinctiveness of different communities in a "one-size-fits-all" identity, thereby endangering "the character proper to each people." When truth is construed too narrowly in terms of rationality alone, such as took place paradigmatically during the Enlightenment, there is always a danger that purely rational findings will undermine or be dismissive of previous ways of understanding the world. It was for this reason that the Enlightenment was in many ways so destructive of tradition, even in a mere secular sense, as we saw in Edmund Burke's reservations about a focus on reason, or truths of reason abstracted from history and cultural identity, undermining "the general bank and capital of nations and of ages," and undermining the "latent wisdom" of tradition.[18]

The analysis of chapter 2 thus concluded that *Gaudium et Spes* highlights the threat that the development of one virtue in modern culture threatens to drown out another. Namely, *scientia*—the ability to discern the truth about things through rationality—threatens to drown out another, namely wisdom, *sapientia*. Now, there are good grounds to suggest that Ratzinger's understanding of truth is closer to traditional *sapientia* than disembodied, Enlightenment truth, for, as we have seen, he considers cultures to develop organically over vastly lengthy periods of maturation, and that these cultures are always already configured somehow by "the prior question of God." For this reason, we suggest a modification to Ratzinger's descriptions of interculturality based on truth, and suggest that we are speaking, here, of something closer to "truth in wisdom," that *sapientia* classically defined by Thomas: "use of right reason concerning God."[19] This leads to a view of interculturality in which there can be an intertwining between Catholic teaching and the great storehouses of wisdom of human cultures, without a danger of a too self-assured confidence in our current perceptions of reality drowning out the accumulated fruits of the past. And here again, of course, we are led to consider the Marian pattern emerging through evangelizing with interculturality.

MARY AS THE SEAT OF WISDOM

The foregoing analysis makes clear that sowing the seed with interculturality requires a grounding rationale or basis, and that this basis—building on Ratzinger's discussion—is best construed as wisdom. The formative or corrective potential of Mary's title, Seat of Wisdom, of course, emerges here, pointing to the Virgin as a paradigm or pattern for evangelizing along these lines. Therefore, in closing, let us elucidate this further by focusing on resources provided for us by the distinctive patronage of this title itself.

Mary as Seat of Wisdom is related to the overarching theme of this book, the Star of Evangelization. This is because Mary as the Star has clear roots in the story of the Magi coming to adore the infant Christ at the Epiphany (Matt 2:1–12). The story of the Epiphany is also the root of the title Seat of Wisdom. The image of the Magi visiting the infant Christ is one of the oldest scenes artistically represented in Christian tradition, appearing from at least the third century in the catacombs in Rome.[20] These images tend to have Mary seated, or enthroned, with the infant Christ on her lap. During the seventh and eighth century, an interesting development occurs, in that images of Mary enthroned with Christ on her lap appear in which the Magi are no longer present. By the tenth century, freestanding statues of Mary thus seated emerge, with the earliest recorded at the Cathedral at Clermont in 946. Around this time, the title of Mary as Seat of Wisdom appears in Christian literature.

The reasons why this title relates to these images and statues is that the Magi are also known as "wise men." But importantly for us, they are wise men who, using the means of disclosing truth in their own worldviews, namely their own ancient religious practices of star mapping and seership, enable them to discern, in an incomplete and murky fashion, some true indications about the birth of the Messiah. They are thus attracted to Jesus and draw toward him, and in this sense, they serve as a cipher for the ways in which a host culture can organically intertwine with the teaching of Christ and his Church in interculturality.

However, it is important to state that in the ancient and medieval images of Mary as Seat of Wisdom, she is not merely enthroned, but is also a throne herself: she is herself a *seat* of wisdom. The roots of this lie deep in tradition, including the highlighting of Jesus as occupying the "throne of his ancestor David" at the annunciation (Luke 1:32), a point included in the first full-length proclamation after Pentecost by St. Peter, who states that God swore to David that one of his descendants would succeed him on his throne (Acts 2:30). This seat on which Christ finds repose, this basis of his earthly life, is thus related to biological development over time; Jesus doesn't just fall from the sky like an extraterrestrial, but, through Mary's DNA, he is deeply rooted in the soil of a certain people and the product, in some way, of a careful and arduous process of providential preparation. In tradition, Mary as Christ's "seat" is also linked to typological readings of the Old Testament linking Solomon with Christ. King Solomon as the paradigm of wisdom is thereby linked by tradition with God's Wisdom himself, Jesus Christ. Solomon's ornate and magisterial throne is wonderfully described in Scripture (cf. 2 Chr 9:17–19), and it is easy to appreciate why this place where Solomon reposes, the basis from which he dispenses wisdom, became connected to the place on earth where Christ reposed, the place he inhabits or is accommodated. For this reason, in a hymn written by Hugh of St. Victor (d. 1180), the Virgin is revered as "the throne of Solomon."[21] Moreover, there are occasions where Solomon's love, the queen of Sheba, is considered a type of the Magi, a wise and exotic creature coming from a distant land to adore the king. For just as the queen of Sheba pays homage to Solomon on his throne, the Magi come to pay homage to the Lord enthroned on Mary.[22]

In the development of images and understandings of Mary as Seat of Wisdom, we can now discern the resources available for our exploration by considering how she exemplifies interculturality. First, the discernment of truth in a culture exterior to Christianity is shown paradigmatically in the Magi, and intertwined—as Ratzinger claims is inevitable—with their religious practices and traditions. Second, the Christ who is encountered in his fullness is found seated, based, enthroned, or supported on the figure of Mary, who, connected with the throne of David, thus signifies Christ's ancient lineage over time in a specific people, just as Catholic teaching of Christ and his Church is intertwined with specific historical developments and cultural elements. Third, and perhaps surprisingly, through the links with King Solomon and the queen of Sheba, we find allusions that resonate with the *inter-* of interculturality, the intercourse or thoroughgoing interchange, linked with erotic symbolism, between two paths of wisdom that meet and fuse into flourishing new forms that bear plenteous fruit. This is seen by calling to mind the profound union between Solomon and the queen of Sheba, immortalized in the beautiful poetry of the Song of Songs. We thus appreciate now that interculturality, proceeding in line with Mary's title as Seat of Wisdom, unlocks dimensions to sowing the seed that promise to inform deeply and structure the way this strategy of evangelization should proceed.

Nonetheless, there is one straightforward and perhaps obvious drawback of Ratzinger's approach yet to be considered. This drawback is particularly pertinent for the contemporary Western scene. Ratzinger's writings discussed in this chapter were, of course, given to those within the auspices of the Church, in whom the presupposition that Jesus Christ is the ultimate disclosure of truth is firmly rooted. We might well ask how this presupposition would carry weight in cultures that have fundamentally questioned the truth of Christian revelation, namely "post-Christian" cultures, such as those that arguably pertain most perceptibly in certain Western European countries. But there is a more fundamental problem even beyond this, for in recent decades there has occurred a deep and far-reaching questioning that anything is, in a sense, *true* in the way described earlier. This is most clearly seen in forms of postmodernism and relativism, which seem to stop any attempt at evangelization dead in its tracks by holding that truth itself is a will-o'-the-wisp, something simply beyond the remit of human capabilities. This problem will be considered in the next chapter.

Chapter 4

Beauty

Mary as "Mystical Rose"

OUR DISCUSSIONS OF Pedro Arrupe and Joseph Ratzinger were each focused on a different side of Paul VI's central axis of evangelization. In examining Arrupe in chapter 2, we emphasized the first side of the axis, presenting the faith as understandably and persuasively as possible. Inculturation works by seeking to incarnate the gospel message in the terms of a "host" culture, in forms and expressions appropriate to that cultural setting. Obviously, this will be understandable and persuasive to those who are themselves formed by that setting, for the gospel message will make sense if expressed "through" someone's cultural "web of significance," and deeply credible, similarly, if presented as the intrinsic essence of that culture.

However, critical questions confronted our reading of Arrupe, particularly with certain presuppositions underlying inculturation, so we examined an approach to evangelizing culture that lays more emphasis on the other side of Paul VI's axis: maintaining the faith in untouchable purity. The key critical issue with Arrupe is the presupposition that Christian life and culture can be separated, and Ratzinger's contention that culture is, by definition, religious proves itself to be a more convincing position. But this conviction, in turn, presents the possibility that evangelization might become a merely haphazard cultural fusion between two religiously formed cultures. Ratzinger's focus on truth as the basis or grounding rationale for any blending of cultural elements in evangelization is a fruitful way of responding to this, albeit with the modification of approaching truth in terms of wisdom.

At this juncture, we are again faced with a critical question, this time surrounding the contentious concept of truth, which has been subjected to philosophical and cultural critique in recent decades. In our contemporary context, where truth itself is held in question, the resplendent light of Christ that refracts from maintaining the creative tension of *Gaudium et Spes* gives forth a different beam, shining outward at a new angle. Here, we move from considering evangelization in terms of "truth in wisdom" to considering it in terms of *beauty*. This presents a strategy for evangelizing in settings inimical to the very possibility of truth. Again, hidden depths of Mary as Star of Evangelization will continue to emerge, this time through her ancient title "Mystical Rose." In ancient liturgy and devotion, Mary is linked with beauty from time immemorial. *Beautiful* is *pulchrum* in Latin, and devotion to Mary as the one who is "all fair" (*tota pulchra*) is well established by tradition. Moreover, the compelling beauty of Mary is always tinged with sorrow, from her being forewarned that a sword would pierce her soul (cf. Luke 2:35), to her agony on Calvary, a scene firmly fixed in popular devotion: "at her cross her station keeping, stood a mournful mother weeping." The rose is, of course, a supreme symbol of beauty, with deep metaphorical richness arising from the thorny stems of the rosebush, capturing something of the bipolarity of visceral human experience, ever caught amid joy and sorrow. This is found particularly in relation to love, whereby joy and sorrow are surely found at their most intense. The duality between delicate beauty and piercing thorns, of course, resonates with Mary, a pure flower whose heart is pierced with sorrow, and it can also be connected (albeit more tangentially) with Paul VI's axis of evangelization. For the beauty of the rose is compelling, and yet the prick of its thorns is sharp and uncompromising; and thus, we might understand evangelization through beauty as both compelling and uncompromising.

We will now examine some specific aspects of the theology of Hans Urs von Balthasar, the foremost theologian of beauty, who provides the theoretical underpinning for evangelizing along the "way of beauty" or *via pulchritudinis*. First, let us briefly situate this chapter in relation to the preceding ones. For our purposes, von Balthasar's understanding of the apprehension of beauty has enormous potential, because that which is beautiful can be understood as both compelling and uncompromising. That is, when confronted with beauty, a human being is "caught-up" in the beautiful object, and "drawn in" to its influence, and so it is compelling, or in von Balthasar's own words, there is an "enrapturing power" to the beautiful.[1] Yet, for reasons that will be disclosed shortly, von Balthasar maintains that beauty is not dictated by personal taste or inclination, but is something genuinely objective, for, in gazing on the beautiful, one is removed from the sphere of vested interests. In precisely this sense, beauty promises to offer an uncompromising means of communication or disclosure. The double-sidedness to beauty—its ability to be both compelling *and* objective—shows how the *via pulchritudinis* enables us to bind the two sides to Paul VI's central axis of evangelization together more closely than we have up to now. That is, if beauty is compelling, then transmitting the gospel message through the beautiful will involve making it understandable and persuasive; it will "draw people in." Yet, if beauty is genuinely objective, then transmitting the gospel message through the beautiful will also enable us to maintain the faith in untouchable purity. Thus, the true and objective reality of Christian faith, if expressed in beautiful form, might not be subject to the danger of overaccommodation and, ultimately, falsehood and heterodoxy, which can result from overemphasizing the need to make the faith understandable and persuasive.

Here, we might well ask what it would mean to evangelize along the *via pulchritudinis*. To flesh this out a little, let us think of the great works of Christian art, like the paintings of Michelangelo, Fra Angelico, or Caravaggio, or maybe architectural masterpieces like St. Peter's Basilica or Santiago de Compostela. As a means of evangelization, examples like these transmit the gospel message—they communicate the reality of Christ and his Church—in ways mere words and assertions perhaps cannot achieve. There is no doubt that countless people have been radically transformed through chance encounters with items of great beauty like these. Perhaps there is no better or fuller expression of the evangelizing power of the *via pulchritudinis* than the liturgy of the Church, which, at best, "draws people in" and "opens them up" to the objective reality of Jesus Christ through the solemn beauty and majestic expression of humanity in rapturous devotion to God.

HANS URS VON BALTHASAR

Hans Urs von Balthasar is an extremely complex theologian, and his work is not easy to comprehend. For example, his most well-known work, *The Glory of the Lord*, is seven volumes, and two other key works, *Theo-Logic* and *Theo-Drama*, are three and five volumes, respectively.[2] This means, of course, that we cannot cover his entire theology in depth in this chapter, and must focus instead on some features of his theological aesthetics that are salient for our purposes. Before doing so, there are three aspects of his life and work that provide a basic orientation for what follows: first, the remarkable level of cultural appropriation of von Balthasar's own German-speaking context (the cultures of Switzerland, Austria, and Germany); second, his close relationship with John Paul II and Joseph Ratzinger in relation to his growing influence on theology from the 1990s, particularly; and third, his centralizing of beauty for theological discussion.

Balthasar was born in 1905, and studied at the Universities of Vienna, Berlin, and Zurich, perhaps the most important universities of Austria, Germany, and Switzerland, respectively. Through his involvement with these three institutions, he became well versed in the intellectual climate of the German-speaking countries. Moreover, his early academic work, not being focused only on strictly theological matters, shows that his intellect could range over a vast sweep of subjects and concerns, including philosophy, literature, art, and music. On this matter, Benedict XVI amusingly relates in *Last Testament* that "when one wanted to select him to vote for anything in the theological commission" he always said "I'm no theologian, I can't do that."[3] His doctoral thesis was titled "The History of the Eschatological Problem in Modern German Literature," showing his aptitude for understanding his own "host" culture beyond the explicitly Catholic domain, for much of the "modern German literature" about which he wrote was not self-consciously religious or theological. Moreover, his first published work, *The Apocalypse of the German Soul*, while building on his doctoral work, drew on a highly complex line of German philosophy, much of which has been considered antithetical to Catholic teaching by many, including such thinkers as Hegel and Kant.[4] So, from early on, Balthasar was (as described by Marc Ouellet), "endowed with a musical ear capable of transposing spontaneously from one cultural register to another" and therefore "above all an interpreter of Western culture."[5]

However, Balthasar was not merely a cultural commentator, but a Catholic priest and—despite his protestations to Benedict XVI—a theologian of high standing. He entered the Society of Jesus in 1928, and was therefore trained in preconciliar Catholic theology, but left the Jesuits in 1950 to establish a "secular institute" called the Community of St. John with an associate of his, Adrienne von Speyr, whom he considered an exemplary mystic, and whose life he felt could not be separated from his own work. He published an astounding number of books, and gained immense renown particularly toward the end of his life. The point to glean from this subsection is that the range of Balthasar's thought covered all manner of cultural expression, which he understood in remarkable depth, without impinging on his status as a thoroughly Catholic theologian. For this reason, Henri de Lubac famously stated "this man is perhaps the most cultivated man of his time. And if one were to find a Christian culture anywhere, one would find it in him."[6] This further demonstrates why von Balthasar is such a highly promising interlocutor for our discussion, for if he understood culture so deeply—precisely from an unflinchingly Catholic perspective—then we can profitably turn to his work to deepen our understanding of culture in relation to evangelization, for in him we find—so de Lubac claims—what is perhaps the very telos of effective evangelization: "Christian culture."

Balthasar, John Paul II, and Joseph Ratzinger

Although von Balthasar is widely acknowledged today as hugely influential on contemporary Catholic theology, throughout much of the twentieth century he was more tangential than high-profile theologians like Henri de Lubac, Karl Rahner, Yves Congar, among others. This was partly because he left the Jesuits, and so lacked the support of an order, carving a highly particular path. However, since that period, he has come to be regarded as one of the leading lights of twentieth-century thought, perhaps even more than some of the other theologians just mentioned.

For reasons we will discuss shortly, this is no doubt due in part to the fact that the two consecutive papacies of John Paul II and Benedict XVI were deeply informed by Balthasar's thinking. This can be demonstrated by John Paul II's insistence on making him a cardinal, in 1998, and Ratzinger's comment at Balthasar's funeral: "It is not merely in some oddly private way that the Church declares to us that Balthasar was a true master of the faith, a sure guide to the sources of living water. But, rather, the Church says this by virtue of her official ministry."[7] Ratzinger, himself, obviously shared von Balthasar's intellectual heritage in the German-speaking world, and affectionately referred to him as a "friend,"[8] explicitly drawing on his teaching at various points. Nonetheless, as already noted, Balthasar takes us into different territory from our discussion of Ratzinger in the previous chapter, due to the latter's centeredness on truth. Let us now briefly introduce von Balthasar's concern with beauty, before analyzing it in more depth, in relation to culture and evangelization.

Balthasar and Beauty

Central to von Balthasar's work is, of course, the theme of *beauty*. The theoretical underpinning of this will be covered in detail later, but for now let's gain some background. First, Balthasar argues that the place of beauty in the understanding of God, the world, and humanity has been progressively undermined in the development of Western civilization, and has been dwarfed by the place of the good and the true. The Good, the True, and the Beautiful were three attributes of Being for the philosopher Plato, and they configured philosophical and theological discussion for centuries. To give a very basic pointer as to their meaning, each became important in medieval theology and philosophy as a subgroup of what are termed "transcendentals": qualities that were said to pertain to being, particularly the being of God—and that were rooted in the transcendent: aspects of God's greatness and majesty. God *is* the good, the true, and the beautiful, their origin and source—"beauty… is identical with Being"[9]—and all that we experience as good, true, or beautiful is ultimately rooted in him. This means that in encountering goodness, truth, or beauty, one *sees* or glimpses something of God *in* the created world.

Balthasar claims that the place of beauty has been undermined in Western thought through a widespread focusing on the good and the true, an undermining of the beautiful by concentrating on ways of understanding morality (philosophical ethics and moral theology), that is, the good; and seeking to understand the true reality of the things of the world (science—particularly cosmology—and epistemology), focused on the true. He argues that there has been a "growing loss" of the ancient perspective that considers the proper station of beauty to be coequal with the good and true.[10] In answering the question as to why von Balthasar considers this decline in understanding of beauty to have taken place, he clearly lays the blame partly at the door of modern rational inquiry. The increasing specialization and separation of the faculty of reason from the complex tapestry of human experience, with its inevitably systematic manner of proceeding, brings with it processes helpfully enunciated by Newman as "cataloguing, arranging, [and] classifying."[11] Reason seeks clarity in pursuit of truth, and this requires a systematic ordering of the components of whatever is being inquired about. Hence, von Balthasar comments that beauty "is a word from which religion, and theology in particular, have taken their leave and distanced themselves in modern times by a vigorous drawing of the boundaries."[12]

But the increasing prevalence of reductive, rational inquiry is itself not enough to explain why beauty would be undermined or sidelined, for there seems to be a quality of beauty that, for von Balthasar, makes it less intellectually tangible than discerning truth or goodness. This is seen by his comment that "beauty is the last thing which the thinking intellect dares to approach, since only *it* dances as an uncontained splendor."[13] With this assertion, von Balthasar points out that beauty is a quality far harder to pin down than truth and goodness, no doubt partly due to its immunity from grounding argumentation, as something that cannot be proved or grounded in the same way as the other two. In that sense it is "uncontained." That is, one cannot prove that something is beautiful in the same way one can provide grounds for something's truth or goodness. One might respond, here, by arguing that beauty is subjective, or a matter of mere fancy, but, as we will see, this is the exact opposite of what von Balthasar maintains. Rather, it is because the splendor of beauty is "uncontained" by human means of argumentation, that he holds it can open us up to divinely revealed reality, a reality not dependent on a human grounding, and in this sense, it can bring us to true exteriority or objectivity.

Before we look more deeply at this, it is important to state that von Balthasar is not aiming to usurp the importance of the true and the good; he states from the outset of his work that he wants "to complement the vision of the true and the good with that of the beautiful (*pulchrum*)."[14] There are certain reasons why von Balthasar argues that beauty is an essential aspect to our understanding of God and the world, or rather our understanding of God's revelation. Later, we will discuss three of these aspects directly concerning evangelization, but, first, it is necessary to look more deeply at the view that Western thinking is undergoing a crisis of truth and goodness. In fact, for von Balthasar, this will show just how interdependent these three transcendentals are, to the degree that he can argue the crises of truth and goodness are—at least partly—a symptom of the progressive loss of beauty's proper place in Western thought: "our situation today shows that [beauty] will not allow herself to be separated and banned from her two sisters without taking them along with herself in an act of mysterious vengeance."[15] This "act of mysterious vengeance" can be approached as the crises of truth and goodness respectively, for von Balthasar maintains that, without beauty, "the good loses its attractiveness, the self-evidence of why it must be carried out," on the one hand, while "the proofs of truth have lost their cogency," on the other.[16]

THE "CRISIS OF TRUTH"

The philosophical and cultural questioning of truth has been of concern for Catholic theology in recent decades, paradigmatically expressed in John Paul II's encyclical *Veritatis Splendor*. There, John Paul II speaks of a "crisis of truth" arising from views, held by some, that human freedom can be exalted "to such an extent that it becomes an absolute, which would then be the source of values" (§32). This means that the freedom to *determine* what is true and good is paramount, that what is true can be assessed based on what is true "for me" or "my truth," and that there is no objective criterion of validity beyond the perspectives of certain individuals or groups. John Paul II considers this thinking to constitute a "crisis," because by this reckoning, genuinely objective truth and goodness are not considered absolute, transcendent, and fixed, but concepts that can be defined however someone might choose (in "freedom") to define them. In short, John Paul II argues against subjectivism (making truth and goodness purely subjective, with each to their own) and relativism (the view there is no absolute truth and goodness for human beings, considering these always to be entirely relative to an individual's perspective).

Before discussing what implications this crisis of truth might have for Ratzinger's "interculturality," it is worth noting how closely bound up truth and goodness are in *Veritatis Splendor*. This is most apparent in the discussion on conscience in article 32. There, we read that, within the crisis of truth,

> the individual conscience is accorded the status of a supreme tribunal of moral judgment which hands down categorical and infallible decisions about good and evil. To the affirmation that one has a duty to follow one's conscience is unduly added the affirmation that one's moral judgment is true merely by the fact that it has its origin in the conscience. But in this way the inescapable claims of truth disappear...so much so that some have come to adopt a radically subjectivistic conception of moral judgment. (§32)

The basic point to note, here, is that if truth is considered to be dependent on an individual's subjectively held convictions, then that individual will not only fail to recognize objective truth, but also objective goodness. For such an individual, only he or she can decide what is good and what is evil; and for John Paul II, this threatens deeply destructive consequences, not only in terms of philosophical theory, but concretely in the everyday life of the faithful, for where truth dies, he tells us, morality must follow.

Before bringing Ratzinger back into our discussion here, let us highlight the scriptural sources for the position outlined in *Veritatis Splendor* by showing how central truth and goodness are to the gospel message. We have seen that Jesus Christ is the bringer of "grace and truth" (John 1:17), the truth that "will make you free" (John 8:32), that God wants "everyone to be saved and to come to the knowledge of the truth" (1 Tim 2:4), that Jesus himself is "the way, and the truth, and the life" (John 14:6), and he imparts his Spirit to us, the "Spirit of truth" (John 14:17). A similar centrality can be accorded to goodness, for who is Jesus Christ but the one who brings forgiveness from sin, and enables life to be reordered in accordance with God's will? Jesus is the one who says, "Do not sin again" (John 8:11), and instructs his followers in the path of true righteousness, most fully articulated in the Sermon on the Mount (Matt 5—7). In fact, regarding evangelization, to pass on the good news of Christ is precisely to say that Jesus Christ is truth, the full revelatory disclosure of God the Father, who is ascended in glory and rules the cosmos. Moreover, to pass on this good news is to offer people his promise that they might no longer be ruled by the power of sin, by acknowledging the error of their ways and perpetually surrendering to God's redemptive power in the sacramental life of the Church, striving after holiness under the admonition to be perfect, as their heavenly Father is perfect (cf. Matt 5:48).

Now, having drawn out some of the detail of *Veritatis Splendor*'s "crisis of truth," and the seriousness of its implications for Catholic teaching and evangelization, we can ascertain that, in cultures deeply marked by the crisis of truth—particularly some of the more philosophically and culturally informed domains of contemporary Western culture—evangelization is faced with major challenges. If people only recognize as "truth" their own subjective convictions, how can we communicate that Christ is "the way, and the truth, and the life"? If, as John Paul II points out, the "crisis of truth" in turn undermines goodness, how can we communicate the "exceptional" righteousness of Christ (cf. Matt 5:47)?

It is in view of this crisis of truth that we will now examine an alternative strategy to that of interculturality, which depends on Ratzinger's centralizing of the "directedness to truth" of cultures for offering a basis on which to evangelize. We will explore the theoretical underpinning of the *via pulchritudinis*, to show that evangelizing through *beauty*—rather than only truth and goodness—can be seen to be particularly appropriate for

BEAUTY AS COMPELLING
AND OBJECTIVE

At the beginning of this chapter, I asserted that von Balthasar understands beauty in a way that promises to bind together the two sides of Paul VI's central axis of evangelization more closely than has so far been the case. On the one hand, if we find something beautiful, it will be compelling—captivating our attention and making a significant impact on us—and will thus be "understandable and persuasive." On the other hand, however, von Balthasar tells us that beauty is genuinely objective, and therefore promises also to preserve the faith in its untouchable purity. The promise of von Balthasar for this inquiry, then, is to provide a strategy for evangelizing that will threaten neither to overemphasize the cultivating of *a response to evangelization* and downplay the imparting of its content (through fostering the beautiful), nor to overemphasize the imparting of its content through *the call of evangelization* and downplay the need for that call to be properly heard and genuinely responded to. To assess if this promise will be fulfilled, we now need to look at the conceptual analysis behind von Balthasar's work to evaluate the substance of his position.

The assertions so far have obviously involved some bold claims, especially regarding beauty as objective. After all, is not the word *beautiful* one of the most subjective of things, in the way that one person might like a certain food, and another loath it, or one man might consider his wife beautiful, and then be shocked to learn his neighbor thinks the opposite? Therefore, we must now see why von Balthasar firmly holds that we should disabuse our minds once and for all of seeing beauty as subjective, a view aptly portrayed in the well-worn English phrase, "beauty is in the eye of the beholder," or in von Balthasar's terminology, "man's habit of calling beautiful only what strikes *him* as such."[17]

Beauty as Compelling

Let us first discern why Balthasar holds that beauty is compelling, and therefore, why it is valuable in pointing to a mode of evangelization along the *via pulchritudinis* that can transmit the faith in an "understandable and persuasive" way. As with the foregoing example of a man who finds his wife beautiful while his neighbor thinks the opposite, the first point to consider is that people find something beautiful that they *love*. Balthasar therefore maintains that to consider something beautiful is to consider it "a loveworthy thing."[18] As Marc Ouellet states, "Christian revelation [is] the absolute love which appears in Jesus Christ" that "ravishes the assent of the believer well beyond his own needs," and "the Glory of God" is "divine love."[19] If, as von Balthasar claims, God is the ultimate root of love, or "absolute love," and we are captivated by this love if God reveals himself to us, encountering God will therefore involve encountering beauty, for we love that which is beautiful, and love is the only appropriate response of someone confronted by "absolute love."

As love is how people respond to God, who is himself love (cf. 1 John 4:8), the gospel message should communicate and foster love, and von Balthasar maintains that this is done through beauty. This has two further ramifications, the second of which will lead to our examination of the objectivity of beauty. First, we can return to our discussion of truth and goodness: for cultures deeply affected by the "crisis of truth," the very notion of plausibility itself has been fundamentally thrown into question. If people genuinely hold there is no real, objective truth, as we have seen, there seems little point in proclaiming Christ is "the truth" (John 14:6). Evangelizing by focusing solely on truth depends on the recipients of evangelization presupposing that there are grounds of plausibility, and it is precisely this that is rendered so troublesome by the crisis of truth. Indeed, for someone like John Henry Newman, even before the crisis of truth has taken hold, the idea of reasoned argument as something that can foster conversion is seen as questionable in itself. This is not only because Newman considers the mind to be merely one aspect of the rich and complex tapestry of human life, but crucially, because he considers it a facet of human experience that does not direct the will in the way that our affective, emotional responses can. Faith involves, of course, the "submission" of the "will" (*Dei Filius* 3), so it is a person's will that an evangelist needs to focus on. For this reason, Newman famously decried against those who try "converting by a syllogism," that is, with purely logical argumentative exercises like syllogistic reasoning.[20] If we consider, for a moment, how little dependence there is on reasoned argumentation in the most transformative decisions of life, we can glean the value of his position. For example, it would be strange, indeed, if one were to propose to one's future spouse based purely on logical argumentation, rather than on an emotional response leading to loving surrender. In terms of evangelization, von Balthasar's position points us toward proclaiming Christ as the object of our love, and not one who—by logic alone—must be the Son of God made man.

Against this background, we can understand why what Balthasar calls "the plausibility of divine love"[21] can be fundamental, for love grounds truth, and this love is invoked by beauty. In this way, the *via pulchritudinis* promises to offer a strategy of evangelization that can sidestep and even restore some of the damage wrought on culture in the contemporary world. Balthasar states that love is "the form of the virtues" (cf. 1 Cor 13:13: "and now faith, hope, and love abide, these three; and the greatest of these is love"), and therefore, he argues, "love is the form of revelation."[22] In other words, love is not "just *one* of the divine attributes," but it *is* God ("God is love"), and similarly, the human response of love is not merely "*one* of the virtues," but their very form, the greatest virtue and the one that binds the others together. This suggests that, if we can communicate God's love, the *via pulchritudinis* can restore truth and goodness to the place awarded by Catholic tradition as transcendentals in our understanding of God and the world. This immediacy to beauty, its impartation without self-centred mediation, allows von Balthasar to speak of the "self-evidence" of beauty, and more dramatically, of the "flash" of "the lightning-bolt of eternal beauty" and of being "snatched up by the beauty of Christ."[23] In short, the "beautiful brings with it a self-evidence that en-lightens without mediation."[24]

To draw out the second ramification of the assertion that we love that which is beautiful, we need to consider how objects of love appear plausible to us. On a basic level, a person we think is beautiful—in the fullest sense of the term that refers to the entirety of the inward and outward character and deeds—is someone whose words carry authority, someone we feel we should listen to, even when they are challenging or awkward. Thus, evangelizing along the *via pulchritudinis* will communicate the gospel message in ways that are plausible, for it communicates love by way of beauty, and to love someone is always to find someone's best, see the good in someone, and apportion that person your unstinting trust. Indeed, in this context, traditions surrounding Catholic devotion to the communion of saints seem to make a great deal of sense. For someone to be classed as a saint is not merely a reasoned conclusion that he or she is holy based on his or her character and deeds, but rather offers a seal of a certain authority to that person, that he or she can and should be listened to, for, in devoting ourselves to the life of a saint, we are able to share in that saint's love of Christ. Balthasar states, "Those who are invited to pray without ceasing, to find and glorify God in all things…should shine like stars in the universe," a passage about which Ouellet comments, "This mission cannot be accomplished simply by speculative combat in the service of truth."[25] But, if love involves plausibility and offers a complement or an alternative to "speculative combat in the service of truth," the question arises as to how this plausibility might involve something genuinely objective.

"Disinterested" Objectivity

We have seen that the beautiful is compelling, and therefore promises to be "understandable and persuasive." Now, we need to ask why and how Balthasar maintains that beauty is objective, and therefore how the *via pulchritudinis* promises also to preserve "the faith in its untouchable purity." There are two fundamental elements to von Balthasar's position that will enable us to ascertain how and why he holds that beauty is objective. The first arises from the view that beauty is not dependent on any precondition pertaining to the apprehender other than love. Compare truth: to discern that something is true we need to have a preliminary understanding of what truth is (as we have seen), and therefore, that which is disclosed as true is dependent on a prior understanding of truth. The plausibility of truth is dependent on human presuppositions, but God's revelation far exceeds what humanity can discern for itself and, therefore, should not be limited by and dependent on merely human presuppositions. The same principle holds for the good. In atheistic societies, for example, swathes of Soviet Russia, the goodness of Christ (particularly his humility and meekness) would not have been readily understandable, because many people born and raised in that society could no longer easily recognize such things as good. To discern beauty, however, one only needs to be capable of love, and this is something that, for von Balthasar, is located at the very heart of what it is to be human. Beauty does not rely on any precondition except love, and love is a universal and fundamental feature of human life, so this means that disclosing God in the beautiful can disclose God more fully and effectively—at least in our contemporary situation—than with truth and goodness. In this way, the beautiful can disclose what is genuinely *exterior* to humanity, because it is not delimited by human presuppositions. By disclosing the exterior, beauty discloses the genuinely objective. That which is objective is, by definition, that which is the case regardless of whether it is recognized as such by an individual, which has no dependence on subjective factors to hold. If beauty is less dependent on human preconditions than truth and goodness, then beauty is the most objective of the three. Consequently, Ouellet speaks of the way of beauty as offering a way "which leads beyond modernity by defining the credibility of Christianity *on its own terms*."[26]

Second, and more fundamentally, Balthasar draws on philosophical discussions from the domain of aesthetics, which refer to beauty as "disinterested," and therefore as objective. Disinterested in this context does not mean "not caring" or being uninterested, as in the common meaning of the term. Rather, it means that our apprehension of beauty is removed from concrete concerns, and therefore is more objective than the good, particularly. In concrete life, we choose to perform actions we evaluate as good in discerning the right course of action. Now, we do not need to think too long about this to realize that many people choose to perform deeds they genuinely think are right or good, but their vision is clouded by vested interests, distorting their perception of the good. For example, someone might decide that it is best not to help someone in need, because that person may become dependent, or take one's generosity for granted, or maybe that person's suffering is justified because his or her own life choices, and so on. Such considerations are, of course, perfectly reasonable, but where reason (discerning truth) falls short here is in enabling someone faced with this ethical question to ascertain if he or she is acting out of self-interest—namely, a desire not to share time, food, or money. It is this meaning of the word *interest*, concern for a certain outcome, that is put out of view when one apprehends a beautiful work of art, for one has nothing to gain from it. For Balthasar, items of beauty—paintings, poems, or pieces of music—are removed from the sphere of our own interests, particularly our self-centered inclinations, from what we want for ourselves. This is the sense in which he holds that beauty is "disinterested," because we behold beauty in a way less likely to become confused with what we want: "Beauty is the disinterested one."[27] Therefore, he writes, "the highest plausibility is only to be found in the realm of disinterested beauty," and "[since] beauty" is "disinterested" it is not a "product," least of all a product "of some person's need."[28]

Beauty and Form

There is a further aspect to von Balthasar's understanding of beauty that informs our understanding of evangelization, and that is the interrelation of beauty to form. Balthasar points out that the Latin for form or "shape," *forma*, is closely related to a word for beautiful, *formosus*, just as the Latin for "likeness," *species*, is closely related to *speciosus*, "beautiful," again, or "comely." This highlights the simple fact that anything we consider beautiful must have form or shape; it must have manifest appearance. Admittedly, one could explore the possibility of there being a beautiful concept or some other type of invisible beauty, but it would be stretching language a little, to say the least. Regarding evangelization, if beauty is intrinsically interconnected with form, if we must "see" something to behold its beauty, the quality of being beautiful is inseparable from the appearance of the form. Let us take a work of art as close to being unanimously regarded as beautiful as we are likely to get: the interior paintings of the Sistine Chapel. Now, imagine trying to describe or invoke the impression of beauty that comes forth from these paintings without the form, or shape, or appearance of those paintings themselves. For von Balthasar, the impossibility of this task is deeply significant, because it leads to a further dimension of the beautiful. If the beauty of a thing is inseparable from its form, that form is irreducible. To return to the Sistine Chapel again, this means that the whole impression of beauty imparted on the person beholding this artwork cannot be split into components, it cannot be exhaustively reduced. Of course, one can highlight the remarkable detail and craftmanship of, say, the muscles of Adam as God breathes life into him, or the stunning array of luminous color of the sky as it rises from the earth and its incredible symmetry of natural human forms in the scene of the Last Judgement, or even the metaphysical and theological depth of Michelangelo's composition. However, even if one were to collate all these qualities as extensively as possible, the impact made on the viewer of these paintings could not be captured by such reductive analysis. There is an indissolvable, irreducible quality to the beautiful that makes it inseparable from its form; it can only cohere in the beautiful form itself and cannot be imparted apart from that form.

This aspect to von Balthasar's analysis offers something important to evangelizing, or rather, a further advantage to the *via pulchritudnis*. Balthasar says of the beautiful object that "whoever…seeks to 'break it up' critically into supposedly prior components…falls into a void."[29] There is, therefore, an "indissolubility" pertaining to beautiful form, which is not necessarily the case with the true or the good. This means that the proclamation of Christ and his Church on the *via pulchritudinis* is not prone to being responded to selectively. That is, the beholder of an evangelizing work of beauty—one "snatched up by the beauty of Christ"—is not likely to break up the experience and select what is personally appealing, without undermining the impact of the whole. By von Balthasar's analysis, one cannot be impacted by the beauty of the Sistine Chapel if one delineates *only* the use of color as beautiful, and not the composition, or—as is perhaps a tempting option for many tourists—claim the visual qualities of the artwork are beautiful but the metaphysical and spiritual depth are somewhat suspect. The evangelizing power of beautiful art is to impart in an instant—a "lightning flash of eternal beauty"—what would take untold years of reading and listening to discern.

MARY AS MYSTICAL ROSE

We can now bring this discussion of von Balthasar to a close by drawing further on our overarching theme of Mary as the Star of Evangelization. We began this chapter by noting how contexts undergoing a crisis of truth pose a critical challenge to Ratzinger's analysis, which causes another beam of the light of Christ to shine forth from the figure of Mary. Again, we find, here, that one of Mary's titles from the Litany of Loreto is particularly resonant and apposite to our concerns in this chapter: Mary as Mystical Rose. Of course, the rose is an ancient symbol and expression of beauty, due to the passionate and striking red of rose petals, its delicate and attractive fragrance, and the symmetry and order of its form.

This brings us to the first layer of resonance between this ancient title and our discussion of beauty. The *via pulchritudinis* can hold together the two sides to Paul VI's central axis, through the interpenetration of the compelling and the objective, of that which is "understandable and persuasive" and "untouchable purity." The attractive beauty of the rose obviously resonates with the compelling and the persuasive, or even the seductive (cf. Jer 20:7). The objective and the uncompromising side to evangelization is aptly demonstrated by the thorny stem of the rose, which pricks the skin of the unwary, just like the message of Christ in all its richness "cuts to the heart" (cf. Acts 2:37) or even circumcises it (cf. Deut 10:16; Rom 2:29). This "stumbling block" to the proclamation of the gospel can uniquely be joined to its joyful aspects as "good news," through the unique interpenetration of the objective and the compelling in beauty.

The application of the adjective *mystical*, however, is less forthcoming. The word *mystical* is difficult to define in English, as it is used in many ways. Obviously, it is closely related to "mystery," and derives ultimately from the Greek μυω (*muō*), meaning "to close the eyes or lips." This verb came to be associated with those initiated into so-called mystery religions, who were bound to silence about their experiences. In this sense, *mystical* is connected with *silence*, which, in Christian tradition is related to contemplation. Contemplation is, of course, a beholding of the mystery of God, a point where all words run short and one is enraptured by God in wordless love. Devotion to Mary as the mystical rose, therefore, is devotion to the Mary who ruminates silently on the mysteries of God, which, as we read in the infancy narratives of Luke's Gospel, are exclusively revealed to her in Bethlehem, Nazareth, and the temple of Jerusalem. This is resonant with the previous discussion of beauty, because in the indissolubility of form, all words run short again. The manifestation or revelation of God in an item of beauty is beheld in silence and cannot be ensnared in human words. Here, we are reminded of the importance of "seeing" in evangelization, not just hearing (the truth) and doing (the good), but having our eyes opened to the magisterial beauty of God in his "unapproachable light" (1 Tim 6:16).

But we find here, once again, that this title of Mary has hidden depths that take us beyond points of resonance and show how Marian prayerfulness promises to be formative of evangelization itself. To emphasize this, we must touch on one of the likely roots of the title Mystical Rose, from the Song of Solomon: "I am a rose of Sharon, a lily of the valleys" (Song 2:1).[30] These words, in the great scriptural text on love, came to be associated with Mary as the one "who art all fair," not least because the text goes on to say, "As a lily among brambles, so is my love among maidens" (Song 2:2). That is, to proclaim of Mary "thou art all fair," *Tota pulchra es* (from Song 4:1), is based on the understanding that Mary is immaculately conceived: "the original stain is not in thee." In the complexly intertwined thickets of human sin, the endless ditches and ravines of thorn bushes and the desolate wastes, grows this immaculate rose, this beautiful form surrounded by thistles. *Ineffibilius Deus* tells us that Mary's *pulchra*, her being free from original sin, comes about "by virtue of the foreseen merits of Christ." This exemplary bearer of the *pulchra* is thus not mediated by, or dependent on, any worldly conditions that precede it, but comes to be purely from the ultimate beauty of Christ himself. In light of this observation, attempts at evangelization—formed and reformed through Marian devotion—can be seen as being importantly transfigured by Christ himself—by foreseen merits of Christ— and thereby we are saved from the urge to set great store on human work: "You have sown much, and harvested little" (Hag 1:6). That is, to reword von Balthasar's own paraphrase of Matthias Scheeben, through the title Mystical Rose, we can glimpse how evangelization should lead to a "divine 'begetting' in" the "womb" of culture,[31] the coming forth of the Son himself in the midst of human self-expression.

Nonetheless, there are critical points that could be raised to the foregoing analysis. There are undoubtedly resources to be found in von Balthasar's own work to answer them, but we will deal with them by drawing a sharp contrast, through studying another figure through whom the beams of the light of Christ radiate from Mary the Star of Evangelization. In the first place, one might ask if there is a certain danger in a discussion of beauty, insofar as it presupposes a certain level of cultural sophistication. Balthasar's own understanding of the apprehension of beauty in the lives of saints by "the simple Christian"[32] suggests his own work would provide resources to respond to this criticism. But let us point to the fact that, as the discussion stands so far, to speak of beauty in this way presupposes that the addressees of evangelization have both the time and inclination to be concerned with what in English-speaking terms would be called "high culture." What of the poor, the uneducated, those busy working for a living and seeking only to feed their families? We could even raise the question of whether or not mass-market consumerism, the crisis of the good, and digital technology have had detrimental effects on the likelihood of people apprehending beauty as described by von Balthasar.

Less pragmatically and more theologically, we might even raise a question to the discussion of Mary as Mystical Rose based on her immaculate purity as conceived without the stain of sin among the wilderness of the thorns and thistles. For Jesus Christ does not differentiate himself *from* sin straightforwardly, but takes on "the likeness of sinful flesh" (Rom 8:3). Jesus enters the sinfulness of humanity, puts himself at the mercy of sinners, and is crowned *with* thorns and mocked by sinners for his total refusal of the complex power dynamics of human fallenness. We are thus faced with the question of Jesus's surrender to human sin, his obstinate refusal to meet it with worldly power, his desire to live among sinners, and his willingness to be crucified. With this aspect to Jesus's life and work, we are presented with a view of evangelization that might take deeply challenging, even borderline pathological forms—in short, with a "harsh and dreadful" love that feels called to witness to Christ in the most difficult and unpalatable of situations.[33]

Chapter 5

Witness

Mary as "Tower of David"

W E HAVE SEEN THE UNIQUE contribution that concentrating on the *via pulchritudinis* can make to the discussion of evangelization: it holds together the need to make the message as "understandable and persuasive as possible" while preserving its "untouchable purity." This is a significant advantage, which arises from focusing on beauty as a transcendental, thus establishing a measure of continuity between the natural world and the supernatural world of grace, and thereby between tilling the "natural" soil of culture and the divine grace of the "seeds of the Word." Nonetheless, we are faced with certain problems that might affect evangelizing along the *via pulchritudinis* in certain contexts.

First, if evangelizers focus on the possibility that cultural items of beauty can be a vessel for the ultimate beauty of Christ, there is a danger of neglecting Christ's luminous presence in far less comely and alluring settings. Quite pragmatic, economic considerations come to the fore here. At least some elements of what a culture defines as beautiful will unavoidably be ensnared in the status quo of a specific economic system, and be surreptitiously affected by market forces. Moreover, the pursuit of the beautiful—or what we might term "high culture"—is a pursuit of people who are relatively privileged, people with disposable income, leisure time, and a suitable level of education and cultivation.

Second, there is the more radical and challenging question of whether cultural sophistication in and of itself per se threatens to work against the teaching of the gospel. This is to ask whether the cultivation of our natural goods and values, however "good" and "appropriate" they might be of themselves, inevitably fosters a sense of human self-sufficiency and autonomy. Culture is, after all, an attainment of the human spirit, and offers a humanly limited wholeness. This might threaten to push God to the sidelines of life, and encroach on matters that would traditionally have been the sphere of religion: the promise of a flourishing and decent life. This second question is related to the first economic question, insofar as the level of cultural sophistication that threatens to usurp the total claim on us made by Jesus Christ is again likely to be the preserve of those in a position of material privilege. Indeed, this is one way of understanding numerous scriptural references about the intimacy of God's love for the poor, whom he "raises from the dust" (cf. Ps 113:7; 1 Sam 2:8), and to whom Jesus came to bring the good news (cf. Luke 4:18). Of those inhibited by earthly circumstances from humanly oriented cultural flourishing, Paul VI speaks about "a thirst for God which only the simple and poor can know" (*Evangelii Nuntiandi* 48; cf. *Evangelii Gaudium* 123).

In the final two chapters of this book, we will deal with each of these questions in turn. Each causes a different beam of the light of Christ to shine forth through Mary as the Star of Evangelization, and each of these will be constructively informed by one title of Mary, each centering on the theme of reversing the world's goods by using the image of a tower: "Tower of David" and "Tower of Ivory." In the ancient Near East, a tower was a sign of human strength, regal power, majesty, stability, and might, but it could also indicate the human tendency to try and usurp God's own majesty, quite literally, by reaching into the heavens (see Gen 11:1–9). These titles are thus connected with traditions surrounding Mary as one in whom the world's goods are reversed; true strength and majesty is found in the poor and simple peasant girl from an obscure region of Palestine. The title Tower of David reverses the expectation for the bearer of the lineage of David to sit in state in a regal palace of Jerusalem; it reverses expectations of economic, political power. The title Tower of Ivory, with ivory as an ancient symbol of purity and simplicity, reverses the association of power with pride and self-sufficiency, suggesting that true strength comes through simple humility.

This chapter will unfold some of the depth inherent in Mary's title of Tower of David by considering the reversal of political and economic power through focusing on the life and witness of Dorothy Day, while the following chapter will do likewise for the title Tower of Ivory, through the work of John Henry Newman. Day exemplifies Christian life lived in self-sacrifice and an unstinting self-offering to and for the vulnerable. She serves as an awkward reminder that Christ has a special relationship with those rejected by the dominant norms of any human culture, who are invariably the poorest members of society. In moving into the sphere of cultural rejection, we are again moving away from "tilling the soil," von Balthasar's cohesive unity cleaves apart, and we cast our attention on "sowing the seed." This movement leads to the contention that certain contexts will not be suitable for the subtler mode of evangelizing by tilling the soil, and must therefore involve explicit witness and proclamation of the suffering servant Christ as Lord.

However, calling to mind the association between "sowing the seed" with the *call of* evangelization, and tilling the soil with the *response to* it, Day's pertinent contribution to this study reminds us that our own response to the call of Christ must be perpetually renewed. In Day's distinct approach to sowing the seed, evangelizers themselves are evangelized by self-offering to the poor; and those rejected by a set of cultural norms bear the presence of Christ in a uniquely powerful way that renews the response to Christ's call in those who minister to them. Day's legacy enables us to combine a concern for our *own* response to Christ through sowing the seed by witness to Christ's unconditional love for the poor in a life of self-offering. Through putting ourselves at the disposal of "those who are usually despised and overlooked" (*Evangelii Gaudium* 48), Day's witness to Christ shows how our strength comes through our own abasement, or is "made perfect in weakness" (see 2 Cor 12:8–10). In what follows, we focus, first, on considering Day as an evangelizer, before studying the centrality of Christ's presence in the poor and vulnerable in her life and work. Then the depth of Mary's title Tower of David will be drawn out, discussing how Mary's strength and power depends on her poverty, which enables the light of Christ to shine all the brighter.

DOROTHY DAY AS AN EVANGELIZER

Dorothy Day's life has been well documented,[1] so this first section need only specifically comment on her witness as an evangelizer. This will show how Day should be understood as a "sower of the seed," notwithstanding the fact that she is not necessarily associated with evangelism in the Catholic mind. Day stands as an awkward and challenging figure in twentieth-century Catholicism,[2] which perhaps explains why she is commonly interpreted as seeking primarily to change or reform the Church. There are good grounds to suggest, however, that the primary focus of Day's life and work was not so much to change or reform, but rather inform and catechize both those inside and outside the flock. The "content" of her message, in this connection, is the unconditional love of Christ for the poor, and the inestimable resources for dealing with social problems lying dormant and untapped in the Catholic tradition. In this sense, I suggest, she should be considered an evangelizer, one who sought to proclaim and bear witness to the good news that the Church as a social program and that Scripture and Tradition are centered on a love for the poor.

To emphasize this point, let us recall the founding of the Catholic Worker Movement. On May Day 1933, against the background of the Great Depression, a massive rally took place in Union Square, New York. In attendance were various groups involved in the labor movement, which were vying for supporters for their respective solutions to the economic crisis. These different factions circulated pamphlets, and among these papers being passed from hand to hand in the crowd, a newspaper appeared that was markedly different from all the others. It was called *The Catholic Worker*, and was written by Dorothy Day and some of her friends, each of whom took positions among the crowd to distribute copies to the people. *The Catholic Worker* newspaper must have raised a few eyebrows on that day. It had an agenda standing in sharp contrast to nearly everything else promising to deal with mass unemployment, poverty, and social injustice. The editorial of that first edition makes this clear:

For those who think that there is no hope for the future, no recognition of their plight—this little paper is addressed. It is printed to call their attention to the fact that the Catholic Church has a social program—to let them know that there are men of God who are working not only for their spiritual but for their material welfare.[3]

It is difficult to imagine how people must have reacted to this editorial. The Church was vociferously opposed to Marxism and communism, and the left-wing labor movement tended to be equally disdainful of the Church. Nonetheless, the group around Dorothy Day argued that there should be a certain rapprochement between these two enemies, in that the Church was, in their view, first and foremost the Church of the poor and dispossessed, and had ample resources in her teaching to provide responses to the problems driving the groups on the left. This example shows that Day sought to unlock the resources available in Catholic teaching for the popular mind, or, as put by her cofounder of the movement, Peter Maurin, "to make the encyclicals click."[4] This informing or catechizing should be understood as the primary thrust of her life and work, rather than an effort to change Church teaching, except in cases where a neglect of the poor resulted in unfortunate misconstruals and ill-informed practices.[5] As she states herself, "Quit worrying about Popes, Bishops, Cardinals.…It's you who need to change, not them."[6]

However unlikely the idea of a Catholic Worker Movement must have seemed to the readers of that first edition of the newspaper, Day's pedigree as an evangelizer is further demonstrated by considering how this message struck a chord in the American imagination. The first print run of the paper sold 2,500 copies; by the end of 1933, the circulation was 100,000; and in 1936, it reached 150,000.[7] Moreover, the Catholic Worker group did far more besides printing a newspaper. They ran soup kitchens, distributed food to the destitute, and opened Houses of Hospitality providing shelter for the needy. They "caught the imagination of the Catholic community in a way that could not have been predicted."[8] Dorothy Day has been called "probably the most fascinating witness to Christ that America has ever produced," and one commentator, Ashley Beck, suggests that she be seen as "a courageous prophet, anticipating the new directions in which the Holy Spirit has led the Catholic Church."[9] Beck's reasoning is that although many of the views espoused by the Movement were "despised by many Americans, including Catholics," in the 1930s, "much of the general philosophy…of Dorothy Day is now in the mainstream of Catholic life."[10] This can be seen particularly in the explicit opposition to war that has been promulgated by the Church since the pontificate of John XXIII, and also the categorical endorsement of the "preferential option for the poor" by John Paul II.[11] In this sense, the influence of her "sowing of the seed" by informing and catechizing is well established.

Although Day faced many challenges and points of resistance from both inside and outside the Church, by the end of her life, it became clear that her contributions were aptly recognized. In 1967, at the International Congress of the Laity in Rome, she was invited by Pope Paul VI to receive communion from his own hands, only one of two Americans given this honor, the other being an astronaut. In 1970, she traveled to Calcutta, and was presented with a cross by Mother Teresa, who acknowledged Day as an "honorary member" of her Missionaries of Charity. In 1971, she was awarded the prestigious Laetare Medal by the President of the University of Notre Dame, for her long service of "comforting the afflicted and afflicting the comfortable." In 1973, she was given the Frederic G. Melcher Book Award for a compilation of excerpts from her column "On Pilgrimage" in *The Catholic Worker*. She was also invited to become a canoness at a New York Episcopal cathedral, given the Gandhi Award for "Promoting Enduring Peace," and in 1978, received greetings from Pope Paul VI via Cardinal Cooke in New York, and a gift inscribed by Pope Pius XII. Day died in a Catholic Worker house at age eighty-three.

CHRIST IN THE POOR AND DESTITUTE

Day's life and work demonstrates not only that she is a "sower of the seed" through her spreading of the good news of the Church's social program, but that she understands a life of self-offering to the poor to involve the ongoing cultivation of one's own response to Christ by the poor. It is vital for understanding Day to appreciate her understanding of Christ's unique presence in the vulnerable. For Day, Christ himself is found in those rejected by the dominant culture, and one can go so far as to say that it is in their being rejected by the world that Christ can make his home in them. Before exploring this, it is necessary to give some attention to an obstacle that arises in seeking to interpret her writing theologically. Day was not an academic theologian, but a journalist, and this is not to criticize her, but to highlight what is probably an advantage. Not being an academic may well have enabled her to maintain a purity of focus on "action and deed" without getting bogged down in distracting theoretical considerations. Nevertheless, it does mean that her writing is different from, say, Joseph Ratzinger or Hans Urs von Balthasar, and so, to bring her work into the more specialized register of this discussion, we need to provide some basic points of orientation.

Working from her written legacy—a handful of published books, the articles from her newspaper, and her recently published diaries and letters—let us imagine, here, the shape and outlook of Dorothy Day's theology. First, we can apply some general comments about the "shape" of theology by Aidan Nichols. Nichols argues that a "structural element" common to different theologies is the notion of a "central axis." He states, "Every theology takes as its central axis some facet of revelation and tries to relate everything to that." He goes on to describe the peripheral elements in such a structure as being "like planets circling a sun," the sun being, of course, the facet of revelation established as the "central axis." One of the numerous examples he gives of a central axis is Aquinas, whose theology, he claims, revolves around "the idea of the coming forth of creatures from God and their return to him."[12]

In seeking to find a central axis for the work of Dorothy Day, we are in very different territory from the Angelic Doctor. Day was first and foremost a living witness, as is made clear by two quotes she was fond of repeating. The first, from St. Francis, is "we do not know what we haven't practiced."[13] The second, from Thomas à Kempis, is "on the day of judgment we will not be asked what we have read, but what we have done; not how well we have discoursed, but how religiously we have lived."[14] So, with Dorothy Day, one has a vital caveat to bear in mind: discursive knowledge is not the center of gravity in her life and work, but rather an optional, secondary consideration, or maybe even an indulgence. With this caveat in mind, we can return to asking what the central axis of her theology would be. Working from some textual references and accounts of her life, there are good grounds to suggest that at the heart of Day's witness is the practice of "the works of mercy," undertaken primarily in the Houses of Hospitality. The works of mercy are the tasks named by Jesus in the Gospel of Matthew: "I was hungry and you gave me food, I was thirsty and you gave me something to drink, I was a stranger and you welcomed me" (25:35), and so on. These actions are often listed in preconciliar Catholic prayer books and catechisms as a bite-size formula of Catholic praxis: "Feed the hungry, give drink to the thirsty, clothe the naked, shelter the homeless, visit the sick, visit the imprisoned, bury the dead."[15]

In setting up the works of mercy as Day's central axis, we inevitably neglect some other aspects of her concerns, a full discussion of which would detract from the focus of this book.[16] But her own writing provides a good basis for centralizing the works of mercy in understanding her. In one article, she describes "the supernatural love we should bear our fellows" as the "foundation stone" of the Movement, saying, "it is on this we build," and "because of [this] love we embrace...the Works of Mercy, [which is a]...means of sharing our love for our fellows."[17] Even more clearly, there is a comment she makes in an article from May 1936: "The most fundamental point in the Catholic Worker program is emphasizing our personal responsibility to perform works of mercy."[18] And again, in 1964 she writes, "The works of mercy are the main works of our lives."[19] There is also textual support from the secondary scholarship. Beck, for example, states that the "heart of the message of Day...and the Catholic Worker is the boundless love of God for humanity...shared...[with] the poor," and he discusses the house that "fed bread and soup to hundreds each day in the Lower East Side" as "fundamental to the vision of the Catholic Worker."[20] Robert Ellsberg similarly describes the Houses of Hospitality as "the heart of the Catholic Worker." So, based on these descriptions, let us pose the central axis of a theology of Dorothy Day as the practice of the works of mercy.

In his description of different theologies having respective central axes, Nichols mentions that different theological elements in a certain theology's "shape" revolve around that center, like "planets circling round a sun." So, let us now take our own concern with evangelization as an element that must be understood in relation to the center: the practice of the works of mercy. In doing so, something interesting emerges. Although, as discussed earlier, Day certainly qualifies as an evangelizer in the straightforward sense of informing and catechizing those inside and outside the flock about hidden or neglected aspects of Catholic teaching (sowing the seed), she also understands our *own* response to Christ—the tilling of our interior soil—to be done precisely *by* performing the works of mercy.

It is clear from Day's work that she is not preoccupied with evangelizing the recipients of hospitality. Her hospitality arises from the unconditional love of the poor, and were there a strategy or underlying motive of that hospitality, it would impose a condition on it. Moreover, to offer hospitality as a means of evangelizing the poor would involve an "us and them" mentality between practitioner and beneficiary, those who "have" the message and the "have nots" who don't, a mentality that is completely out of keeping with the Catholic Worker Movement. Day and her followers demanded voluntary poverty from all members of their communities, so there is no "us and them," just "us." We are not dealing here with one group of people ("us," or practitioners) being comfortable with their own answers to life's questions and seeking to bring another group of people ("them," or recipients) into line with those answers. Day considers all followers of Christ to be placing themselves at the mercy of his love, and standing in solidarity with each other.

This does not mean that many residents of the Houses of Hospitality were not led to enter the Church, nor that Day and her companions would shrink from discussing Scripture, Tradition, and doctrine with them. But it does mean that, for Day, the "harsh and dreadful love" of Christ that irresistibly overflows into concern for the neighbor can have no agenda or strategy, no conditions. The practice of the works of mercy for the vulnerable neighbor is not merely an instrument serving some other, higher good; it is an end in itself. That said, it is equally clear from Day's writings that the self-sacrificial love of the poor does have profound effects. The important thing for this discussion is that the locus of these effects is not on those welcomed into the Houses of Hospitality, but on those who welcome them. Christ is the "stone that the builders rejected," and through loving those who are rejected he becomes the "cornerstone" (cf. Ps 11:22; Matt 21:42; Mark 12:10; Luke 20:17). Day thus offers a striking understanding of the connection made in Scripture, that the one who is "rejected" is "the Holy and Righteous One" (Acts 3:14), that the one "rejected by mortals" is "chosen and precious in God's sight" (1 Pet 2:4). So, the question arises how this approach to the vulnerable informs this book specifically, or rather, how the interior soil of those treading the path of loving responsiveness to God's will is "tilled"—cultivated, renewed, and prepared—by Christ's presence in those who are rejected, Christ as a "sign that is rejected" (Luke 2:34) by cultural norms.

To answer this question, let us focus on two closely related aspects of Day's understanding of her vocation of lived self-offering to the poor. In the first place, the sheer level of difficulty involved in ministering to the needy in voluntary poverty is seen by Day as a process of mortification. Mortification is of course dying to self, and the key biblical association here is Galatians: "It is no longer I who live, but it is Christ who lives in me" (2:20–21). So, in mortifying the self, the idea is that space is made for Christ. This is fundamental to Day's understanding of her activities. She discusses the difficulty involved in dealing with the various complaints being made by guests in one house in which she lived and worked, mentioning "the grumbling, the complaints, the insidious discontent spread around." But she states "to say nothing" in the face of such issues is "the most difficult of mortifications."[21] At one point, she speaks of desiring to share the sufferings of Christ, mentioning "self-imposed mortifications, [and] self-imposed dying to self."[22] This emphasis is also connected to one of the controversies that affected the group. It was involved in the growth of the so-called retreat movement, which was centered on a particularly rigorous version of the Ignatian retreat. Some Church authorities were concerned about the extremities of mortification involved, but Day argued that "grace is a share in the divine life" and "the law of this supernatural life [of grace] is love," which "demands renunciation." "In mortifying the natural," she states, "iron is transformed in the fire."[23] This metaphor of reshaping or transforming iron in the fire can relate to our own metaphor of tilling the soil. Through dying to self in working against natural instincts that demand security, comfort, and peace, the interior soil of one's own personhood is "dug up" or "turned over," reshaped and prepared so the seed of the Word can take root.

This understanding of mortification in Day's work explains some of the most challenging aspects of her writing, like her love of St. Thérèse of Lisieux's own love of suffering—the "Little Flower" who spoke of being seized "with a passionate longing to suffer," of feeling a "deep, true love for it."[24] St. Thérèse says that "suffering stretched out her arms to me and I embraced her lovingly," and quotes St. Thomas à Kempis, saying, "O God, who art unutterable sweetness, turn to bitterness to me all the comforts of the earth,"[25] for she claims to "find joy in contempt of self."[26] As she states, "One *desires* to share in the sufferings of Christ. One desires to share in the hardships of the beloved, [to] hunger, [and to] thirst, [to practice]…dying to self…we want to strip ourselves and clothe our beloved. We want to fast because of his hunger even [when] we cannot feed him…and this is the folly of [our] love."[27]

The Houses of Hospitality were volatile places, where various social problems ravaged the guests—most obviously alcoholism. They were funded entirely by donations, which would suddenly dry up, and often the buildings were leased temporarily and informally, and possession of the properties had to be surrendered at short notice. Day was thus bound to live in a way that was radically dependent on God's will day by day. In turn, this relates to her fondness for prayerful *supplication*. Supplication is petitioning God. Throughout Day's texts she refers to this— often in a startlingly direct way, with reference to specific items required to perform the works of mercy. A good example of this is her fondness for praying novenas. A novena is a nine-day prayer cycle, based on the nine days the disciples were thought to have waited for the Spirit between the ascension and Pentecost. It is usually prayed to seek the prayers of a specific saint toward fulfilling a specific request. In her autobiography, Day speaks glowingly of this practice. If one novena is not answered, she says, start again from the beginning, and keep going until it is.[28] Maybe she prayed such a novena after May 10, 1958, when she records praying to St. Thérèse of Lisieux "for a suitable building," after being forced to give up a house of hospitality. Either way, it was not until July 3 that a new property was available, and she writes, "God be thanked. St. Thérèse has helped us."[29] Sometimes the supplications are not so specific, such as the cry she offers up on reading of napalm deaths in Vietnam. She writes that, faced with such difficulties, supplication is "the only answer"—

"asking God to increase…faith." The point, here, is that a central axis, with such innate unpredictability and vulnerability as the practice of the works of mercy, lays one open to irresolvability in such a way that the only response is to petition God.

Surprisingly, on this point, we find agreement between Dorothy Day and the very different figure, the Lutheran theologian Dietrich Bonhoeffer. Bringing this moment of agreement to light will enable us to pose a different question to the previous chapter's discussion of Mary as Mystical Rose. In one of Bonhoeffer's most uncompromising passages on the death of the will, he states, "My own will to have my own way by means of prayer must die, [it] must be killed." He does not pull any punches, here, following this up with the sentence, "The word 'kill' must be spoken." He goes on, "My own will has died when Jesus' will alone reigns in me." "And it is then," says Bonhoeffer, that "I can pray that the will of God…be done." For Bonhoeffer, "the only way my prayer is…pure is when it comes from the will of Jesus." "Then," he writes, "prayer [*Beten*] really is *supplication* [*Bitten*]." He also states that "general adoration [*Anbeten*] is not the essence of Christian prayer; supplication is."[30] To move from the "visual" or "mystical" practice of adoration, to the immediacy of petitioning God urgently for help, shows the stark differentiation between the *via pulchritudinis* and the Christian spirituality on offer here. Not least, because, here, the interior soil is tilled by awkward, uncomfortable, painful, and difficult suffering in the name of Christ—in short, by repeated encounters with beauty in the form of rejection, in the form of that considered ugly and unseemly.

MARY AS TOWER OF DAVID

Having established that Day offers an exemplary example of straightforward evangelization through informing and catechizing, and her highly particular approach of voluntary poverty and unconditional love of the poor that serves to till the soil of one's intimate personhood, we can bring this discussion to a close by showing how her life and witness resonate with Mary's title Tower of David and yet can be constructively formed by the place of this title in Marian piety. By centralizing a self-sacrificial love of neighbor in this way, another beam of the light of Christ shines forth from Mary as Star of Evangelization, through the turning upside down of our naturally self-centered concern for survival and self-advancement, by thrusting us repeatedly into situations of ugliness and pain—the reversal of the world's values paradigmatically expressed by Jesus's crowning with thorns. As stated at the outset to this chapter, a tower is a symbol of human strength, regal power, majesty, stability, and might. Day's life and witness resonate with Mary's title as Tower of David, however, by showing how—for an evangelizer—true power, true stability, and true might must belong to Christ alone, just as with Mary, an unlettered, poor, and silent servant of God could become the vessel of the most awesome divine majesty, like the unarmed young man, David, who took on Goliath to the incredulous amusement of his fellow soldiers.

Venerating Mary as the Tower of David should thus shape evangelizers by tilling their soil, reminding them of the importance of suffering, and of Mary as sharing Christ's reversal of worldly powers, which are always culturally formed to some extent. Nonetheless, by pondering this title a little longer, some issues come to light with Day's life and work.

First, although David was a weak and unlikely contender to Goliath, and although his prayerfulness and interior poverty meant he was aided by God, he remains unavoidably linked with political power in that he does, of course, become King David. This highlights the fact that, in Catholic thought, there must be a place for "appropriate" or "proper" political power. That Day understood this is clear, for her own self-definition as an anarchist was sufficiently sophisticated for her to hold firm to Church authority and to defend these she called "popes, bishops, cardinals," who must hold some property rights and therefore be embedded in political and economic power structures. Her own ecclesiology—however unformed and latent—must therefore involve an awareness that the Body of Christ cannot be exempt from worldly power; it cannot always be only countercultural. The challenging question that arises from her work, then, is how the Church should situate itself in relation to worldly power, if it is not to go as far as Newman considered with the "regal" office of Christ being centered on the pope as sovereign along with the Roman curia. For Newman, the office of Christ as King applies to the church as a "political power," and what Newman calls the "principle" of this office is "expedience." To enter into the political sphere, to negotiate action among various sources of power, inevitably involves choosing relative, conditional goods: doing what is best given the circumstances, the closest approximation to the good in each situation.[31] Part of Day's awkwardness is her resolute refusal to enter into considerations of expedience, particularly with the Catholic Worker commitment to absolute pacifism, for example.

Mentioning Newman's understanding of the regal office, here, brings to light a second issue. The uncompromisingly countercultural nature of the Catholic Worker Movement is undoubtedly highly important, and has been deeply effective for evangelizing, as we have seen. Moreover, the interior tilling of the soil by the works of mercy provides a radical understanding of evangelization that should inform many strategies for increasing Church attendance afoot in the contemporary world. But by so resolutely focusing the practice of the works of mercy at the center of everything, one could ask how Day should be oriented in relation to the variety of charisms and gifts so central to Catholic understandings of vocation, stemming from passages in Pauline literature particularly, which speak of a variety of "gifts," "services," and "activities," with which people are graced differently, or individually, in and for the Church community (cf. 1 Cor 12:4ff). This understanding of different gifts in Paul connects with Newman's understanding of the "regal" office, for Newman considers the "regal" calling to be one of three paradigmatic offices of Christ, with which believers are "anointed," the other two being the "priestly" and "prophetic."[32] Day's life and work threatens to present elements from one of these anointed offices as superior over the others, which is exactly what Paul exhorts the faithful not to do: there are "many members," dependent on each other, and all belonging to "one body" (1 Cor 12:20).

That many were evangelized in some way by the Catholic Worker over the years is unquestionable, but one wonders how many could "go the distance" like Day, which, while highlighting her as a contender for "heroic sanctity," also questions the degree to which her approach can offer a broad and inclusive understanding of evangelization with various applications and forms. Perhaps surprisingly, the devotion to Mary as the Tower of David can help us in our response to this issue arising from Day's work. This is because David is an exemplary instance of an "anointed" one (1 Sam 16:13; 2 Sam 5:3), and in this way, he prefigures the *Christos* (meaning "anointed"), whose kingdom is "not from this world" (John 18:36). But Newman's exploration of the threefold office, working from Eusebius's *Ecclesiastical History*, is predicated on different forms of anointing, different appellations of the title *Christos* in the Septuagint, given to prophets and priests as those anointed. For Newman, the faithful are anointed by the Spirit to share in the threefold office of Christ, which famously influenced *Lumen Gentium's* discussion of the laity being anointed with these three offices. But there are a variety of gifts in which not everyone shares, not to mention the variety of circumstances and situational responsibilities that mean that a radically self-sacrificial life can be lived out very differently in relation to those different circumstances.

Therefore, we proceed, now, to the last chapter, which focuses on John Henry Newman, who, in one sense, presents an even more radical position—the possibility that cultural sophistication is problematic in and of itself—but one that has a broader range than Dorothy Day's and is focused on a central virtue of Christian life in which all are called to share: simplicity.

Chapter 6

Simple Assent

Mary as "Tower of Ivory"

IN THIS CHAPTER, we will examine two aspects of John Henry Newman's work. The first issue stems from our discussion of von Balthasar and the danger that the *via pulchritudinis* emphasizes cultural sophistication that could make the faith exclusive to those with a certain level of education, cultivation, and material privilege. In this regard, Newman considers whether cultural sophistication in and of itself, per se, threatens to work against the teaching of the gospel, that is, whether evangelizers should be careful and even suspicious of the "cultivated"—those with a well-developed scheme of human flourishing. On this view, the strength or stability of human nature (natural goods and values) may preempt or circumvent the volatile, transformative power of grace. The issue, here, is that the cultivation of our natural goods and values, however "good" and "appropriate" they might be of themselves, inevitably foster a sense of comfortable human autonomy. The achievements of merely human culture are, of course, attainments of the human spirit, and herein lies their precariousness in relation to the gospel; for the human spirit threatens to push God to the sidelines of life. In response, evangelizers can adopt an alternative stance in relation to cultural sophistication, a stance or "posture" of simplicity, for, as we have seen, there is a "thirst for

God that only the poor and simple can know" (*Evangelii Nuntiandi* 48; cf. *Evangelii Gaudium* 123).

The second issue arises from our examination of Dorothy Day, and the highly specific nature of her witness that threatens to undermine the variety of gifts with which the faithful are anointed by the Holy Spirit. Simplicity will emerge in what follows as a paradigmatic, fundamental, and base virtue of Christian life, by being construed not merely in an economic or material sense. Of course, simplicity is most frequently associated with its material interpretation: living simply without the accoutrements of wealth, prestige, and excess, which is a demand incumbent on all followers of Christ. But here it will be interpreted more broadly as a fundamental disposition of Christian living, a direct, pure-hearted, sincere, and single-minded centrality of Christ's lordship at the very center of life, serving as an apt rejoinder to the problems of cultural sophistication (or complexity).

This discussion of Newman's simplicity is an exploration of a final beam of the light of Christ shining forth through Mary as the Star of Evangelization, coming from the issues with von Balthasar and Day. Here, Mary's title as "Tower of Ivory" will prove central, for ivory is an ancient symbol of purity and simplicity, whose gleaming whiteness is suggestive of the robes worn by the martyrs (cf. Rev 6:11). To be in a position of simplicity is to be pure, purely focused on Jesus Christ. Just as white is a color without hue, so the hearts and minds of the simple faithful are not so much flourishing with the human spirit, but are "emptied out" to be occupied only by the Spirit of Jesus. With this, we will reach an understanding of tilling the soil and sowing the seed that lies at the very heart of life in Christ, a life overflowing into the lives of others, whom God wants to be saved and to come to knowledge of the truth (1 Tim 2:4). The purity, focus, and directness of Newman's "simple assent" offers an example of sowing the seed with broad cultural application, for it fundamentally challenges dangers inherent in the notion of culture itself. But, at the same time, we will build on Day's contribution to this study by applying the notion of "tilling the soil" to evangelizers themselves—the tilling of their interior soil—by widening its scope so it is understood as a central feature of life in Christ. That is, the tilling of the soil, the tilling of the ground for the response to the call of faith, is effectively understood as a call for simplicity, a perpetual renewal of conversion through pure-hearted centeredness on Jesus Christ. The Tower of Ivory will be placed at the beating heart of evangelization, as the place where Paul VI's central axis of evangelization is most compellingly expressed: where the faith is "as understandable and persuasive as possible," and yet, preserves "its untouchable purity," for if the gospel message is communicated from a disposition of Christ-centered simplicity, it will be communicated *simply*, and thus be understandable and persuasive. Moreover, through communicating it simply, we will preserve its "untouchable purity" of being focused purely, or singularly, on Christ alone, without any human adulteration.

ON SIMPLICITY

Before studying aspects to Newman's life pertinent to this discussion, let's first attend to the word *simplicity*, which has various semantic references. The adjective *simple* can be applied to human beings in diverse ways, but it is commonly used in a negative or pejorative sense. To call someone "simple" often means they are basic, intellectually unsophisticated, or even stupid or foolish, as exemplified by the insult "simpleton." However, rather than being pejorative, the *simple* can mean something commendable and desirable. In this sense, to be simple is again to be basic, but rather than lacking anything, it means to be straightforward, uncomplicated, and not pulled this way and that by different influences. This form of simplicity is linked with unity or oneness, for the simple person, in this sense, is single-minded, or has integrity, which comes from the Latin *integer*, meaning "whole."

In the original Greek of the New Testament, the semantic ambiguity of the English word *simple* does not hold. There are different clusters of words for the negative form of simplicity as stupidity, and for simplicity as single-mindedness. Matthew and Luke, for example, use the word ἁπλους (*aplous*) for the single-minded simplicity (or soundness) of the eye that causes the whole body to be filled with light, and Paul uses ἁπλότητι (*aplotēti*) and ἁπλότητος (*aplotētos*) at numerous points, such as when he speaks of the "simplicity that comes from God" (see

2 Cor 1:12; "godly sincerity," NRSV). These words are not, it seems, confused with the words like ἄφρονα (*aphrona*), used when Paul asks no one to think him stupid or a fool.

This distinction is also clear in the Septuagint. This translation of the Psalter, for example, does not confuse the ἄφρων (*aphrōn* or "fool") who has said in his heart, "There is no God" (Ps 14:1) with the "simple hearted," whom the Psalmist says "the Lord protects" (Ps 116:6). The same distinction holds for the Septuagint translation of the Wisdom literature, where words like ἁπλοῦς (*aplous*) and ἁπλότητι (*aplotēti*) frequently crop up, such as in the opening to the Wisdom of Solomon, commending us to seek God in "simplicity of heart" (ἁπλότητι καρδίας—*aploteti kardias*).

In the Vulgate, Jerome renders ἁπλοῦς (*aplous*) and its cognate terms with words like *simplex* or *simplicitus*, and perhaps this move was instrumental in assuring that "simplicity" was a key theme of the Latin tradition, leading one patristic scholar to note that many early theologians, "comprehend under the one word [ἁπλοῦς (*aplous*)/*simplex*] the whole magnanimous and honourable type of character in which…singleness of mind is the central feature."[1] No discussion of simplicity and life "in Christ" would be complete without mentioning the person in whom this theme reaches a crescendo: St. Francis of Assisi. St. Francis is, of course, known as the saint of holy simplicity (*sancta simpliciter*) and the *cor simplex*—the simple hearted. The reasons for this are well known, but it should be acknowledged that St. Francis does confuse matters again by joining together stupidity and single-mindedness. This is shown paradigmatically in his self-description as being "simple and idiotic" (*simplex et idiota*), with *idiot*, here, being not quite as harsh as in modern English, but still meaning "ignorant," or literally in thirteenth-century Italy, someone without a university degree. As challenging as this might be, a scholar of remarkable intellectual sophistication and erudition, Joseph Ratzinger, famously said of St. Francis, "The *simplex et idiota* will triumph over the greatest scholars."[2]

Speaking of the "idiotic," even when remembering its proper meaning in the context of the thirteenth century, will no doubt be somewhat jarring for people learning about theology and well versed in the many complex levels of intellectual sophistication attained by Catholic doctrine. Surely, we are not to throw out all our books and try to forget everything we have learned, for the Catholic tradition teaches us about the right use of reason, which finds its home in God, for "a more penetrating knowledge will in turn call forth a greater faith" (*Catechism* 158). In responding to this point, we need to think of simplicity in terms of *orientation*. If the proclamation of the gospel must go out to the simple (poor and lowly), and to be simple (straightforward and basic) is, in a sense, to be receptive and open to God, while moreover being simple (pure of heart) is closely linked to being holy, then our knowledge and learning must always be *oriented to simplicity*. In other words, we must ensure that, by cultivating the intellect and growing in knowledge of the good, the true, and the beautiful, we seek somehow to remain "pure of heart," and, crucially for an evangelizer, we seek to direct this knowledge appropriately to those with "simple hearts" to whom Jesus was sent to "proclaim the Good News."

Let us now examine John Henry Newman's life to discover why he is suspicious of complexity, and what he considers dangerous about cultural sophistication. This will enable us to outline why he maintains that "simple assent" must orient the heart of theology, so we don't have to throw away our books and start again, but rather foster "simple assent" to Jesus Christ.

BLESSED JOHN HENRY NEWMAN

John Henry Newman is a very well-known figure, both in his own lifetime during the nineteenth century (1801–90), and today. He was beatified in September 2010 by Pope Benedict XVI, during the latter's visit to Britain. For those with an interest in Newman's theology, this did not come as any great surprise. Since his death in 1890, Newman's star has shone increasingly brightly in the Catholic theological firmament. His work has been described as "marking a watershed in the development" of modern theology,[3] and came to fruition, particularly, at the Second Vatican Council; he is often referred to as the "Father of Vatican II."[4] Although Newman is not directly referenced in the conciliar documents (hence his other title of the "invisible peritus"[5]), he provides certain fundamental elements of conciliar theology. Against this backdrop, interest in Newman grew to the point where people began to argue that it "seem[s] appropriate to compare him with Augustine and Aquinas."[6] Ian Ker has suggested that not only will he be canonized, but he will also be recognized as "a 'Doctor of the Church,' that is, a teacher whose writings carry a special authority…far superior to that of the most brilliant and learned theologians."[7]

As with some of the other thinkers we have studied, Newman was a prolific and immensely influential writer, so for our discussion, we need only highlight certain relevant aspects of his life and work. In this case, there are two pertinent points to be made. First, Newman's life trajectory involved an overcoming of his own cultural inheritance and setting, while second, this led to his articulating some challenging positions on the matter of cultural sophistication, for he overcame an intellectual tradition with considerable literary and artistic complexity.

Overcoming Cultural Inheritance

Newman is most widely known in his British homeland as a *convert*. He converted to the Roman Catholic faith in 1845, from the established Protestant Church of England. In the twenty-first century, this move from Anglicanism to the Roman Catholic Church is relatively common, and not especially controversial. In 1845, it was a deeply subversive and controversial act, which was preceded by much inner turmoil and struggling on Newman's part, and had deep consequences for his life and work. Indeed, the fact that today such conversions are relatively common is in part thanks to Newman himself, who trod a path and cleared the way for many to follow in his wake for well over a hundred years.

Before 1845, Newman was an Anglican minister, theologian, and academic at Oxford University. His reasons for converting were obviously theological: he devoted much of his life to studying the Church fathers, and discovered in them that the ancient, early Church was the Church of Rome—in unbroken succession—and his own Protestant denomination was ultimately heretical. He thus realized that, to follow in the faith of the fathers, he needed to convert. Although his reasons were theological, the point to bear in mind is that it had deep cultural ramifications. Newman was a public figure and had gained massive notoriety for agitating within the Anglican denomination and British public life more generally. To indicate briefly what this involved, he was the founder of a movement of Anglican ministers who wanted to ground their denomination on the theology of the ancient Church, and who sought to bolster the relationship between their church and the state, against the forces of modernity and liberalism. This alone indicates how deeply intertwined his thinking was with English culture: with the royal family, the parliamentarian tradition, and its literary and artistic inheritance.

By converting, however, he was immediately consigned to the periphery of this culture. He had to surrender the possibility of working at Oxford University again, for at that time Roman Catholics were not allowed to enroll at the university, let alone teach. He was subjected to much criticism and outright prejudice in the popular press, who condemned him as a traitor who had committed something almost amounting to treason. As a Catholic, his standing as a deeply controversial figure continued, not least around the time of Vatican I, when the doctrine of papal infallibility was fully codified and promulgated. The British establishment assumed that one's first loyalty should always to be one's homeland, to one's own culture and country. If the pope is infallible, they argued, then you must obey him over against the monarch, and this was unacceptable. In the background to these controversies is the deeply troubled relationship between Britain and Ireland. Ireland had, of course, remained Catholic, despite being part of the British Empire. Concerning someone like Newman, there was genuine anxiety that his loyalties would lie more with the Irish than with the British, now he shared their religion.

Importantly, Newman found his inner turmoil before conversion, and his exterior turmoil afterward, deeply troubling. As those who have undergone the experience of conversion in a non-Catholic country testify, one still belongs to one's own country culturally *after* conversion; one's sensibility and disposition are unavoidably formed by that culture, even though one's heart now belongs to the Church. What we see, then, is Newman undergoing an overcoming of his cultural inclinations because of his faith, a heart-wrenching decision for faith over against culture. This is particularly perceptible in his writings from Ireland, unsurprisingly. In studying some of these writings, we will ascertain how Newman battled his cultural inheritance, while he was what he termed "a Catholic Saxon [meaning Englishman] in Ireland," a Celtic land. Here, we can see that by faith he was closer to the Irish, while culturally he was closer to the British, a cultural inheritance from which he recanted.

117

Overcoming Cultural Sophistication

Newman's battles with his own cultural inheritance developed and impacted on his theology in a way that extends beyond mere accidents of history, like his being born British. His struggles with the English establishment, who prided themselves on their rationality and common sense, made him suspicious of cultural sophistication per se, as making people autonomously secure, and closing their hearts to the truth. Moreover, the British establishment was, at the time, the center of a vast empire, the largest the world had ever seen, and so people in this establishment had a sense of their own importance and superiority. Indeed, this is perceptible in many of the struggles with Catholicism, because many British had assimilated into their psyche that it would be improper to be obedient to the pope, on the ground popes were then always Italian. As we will note, the immense sophistication of Newman's Oxford University background became something he saw as an obstacle to faith for many. This has important implications for our concern with evangelization, suggesting that an evangelizer will sometimes have to challenge the complexities of culture, and bring people back to the simplicity of faith. It is against this background that Newman became sensitive to the dangers of book learning, academic knowledge, and any cultural sophistication that has become untethered from the simplicity of faith—the straightforward, single-minded purity of the gospel. We can interpret what he is getting at when he states someone "is only half a man if he can't put his book into the fire when told by authority."[8] That is, the whole person is claimed by faith, and cultural and intellectual pursuits must lead from and toward that faith, so when they threaten to usurp or undermine it, these pursuits must be vehemently discarded.

CULTURE AS "AN INSIDIOUS AND DANGEROUS FOE"

In 1851, the archbishop of Dublin, Bishop Paul Cullen, invited Newman to come to Ireland and preside over the founding of a Roman Catholic University, as university provision in Ireland at the time was mainly Protestant. Here, we focus on a reading from one of the lectures he gave for the opening of this university: "Discourse IX, Duties of the Church toward Knowledge." In the preceding eight discourses, Newman, in his own words, has been "inquiring what a University is, what is its aim, what its nature, what its bearings."[9] Much of this has been taken up with establishing what he calls "Liberal Knowledge." This is not related to "liberalism," as a political theory, but is rather a pedagogical classification for an approach to learning that argues that the intellect should be cultivated for its own sake. There is much discussion to this day about whether education should be primarily about its use for society (vocational), or as something "good in itself" (knowledge for its own sake). Newman argues forcefully that education is "good in itself," because it fosters a "liberal" disposition in the learned, which means a freedom of the intellect from error, falsehood, and the narrow-minded restrictions of prejudice. He thus argues that a mind trained with a liberal education will exhibit a certain liberality—the liberality of a cultivated intellect—with the attributes he lists as "freedom, equitableness, calmness, moderation, and wisdom."[10] An intellect trained in this fashion, he maintains, will not be pulled back and forth by different competing ideas, but will be able to deal with things fairly and with composure, and in this sense, "freely."

This view of education is undeniably English in its origins, and Newman is unapologetic in drawing on his Oxford University days to make his case for liberal education, even though he is speaking to Catholics in Dublin. As well as being rooted in his own cultural setting, this view of education is directly related to a theory of culture, and for Newman, to be cultivated means to have the "goods and values of human nature" brought to fruition. This is, of course, the classical understanding of culture (or *cultura*) on which we focused in our discussion of *Gaudium et Spes* in chapter 1. According to this view, culture should develop and nurture the goods and values of human nature, just as academic work should develop and nurture the goods and values of the intellect ("freedom, equitableness, calmness, moderation, and wisdom"). Returning to the explicit definition of *culture* from *Gaudium et Spes* should also call to mind the implicit approach to culture in this document: cultures can also work for good or ill, and do not always cultivate the good and the valuable. It was, of course, by holding these two together in a creative tension that we saw the light of Christ refracting at different angles, each of which we have explored through the figure of the Virgin Mary.

Newman is ambiguous about culture. But the vitally crucial difference between him and the other thinkers we have covered is not that he thinks that cultures that "cultivate the goods and values of human nature," or "truth," or "beauty," are good, and those that do not are bad. Rather, Newman adopts a radical position that it is precisely *in* the cultivating of the good, the true, and the beautiful, that culture must be handled sensitively. That is, in its enabling of human beings to encounter the truth, to foster and develop that which is good and valuable, culture threatens to drown out faith, to leave human beings confident and secure in themselves, to usurp the need for God to always ground any good we might encounter. In "Discourse IX," therefore, we arrive at a tension like that outlined at the beginning of this chapter, where we discerned that the gospel is essentially based on simplicity, but at the same time is amplified in Church teaching with immense sophistication. For Newman, to be cultivated or sophisticated *should* thus benefit Christian faith, but it can also actually impede it, so we need to ensure it is properly oriented on the simplicity of faith and not something with its own center of gravity, as it were.

For this reason, Newman states that a cultivated intellect (which has been developed and fostered to bring its goods and values to fruition in a liberal education) "concurs with Christianity in a certain way, and then diverges from it; and consequently proves in the event, sometimes its serviceable ally, sometimes, from its resemblance to it, an insidious and dangerous foe."[11] So let us now examine why Newman argues that culture can be "an insidious and dangerous foe," before establishing how we can ensure it remains a "serviceable ally" to faith, or rather, evangelization.

Newman argues that the cultivation of our goods and values (as exemplified in a liberal education) "has a special tendency…when cultivated by beings such as we are, to impress us with a mere philosophical theory of life and conduct, in the place of Revelation."[12] With the comment, "beings such as we are," we can surmise this is a delicate nod to our status as fallen, and it is worth remembering that the fall in Genesis is associated with the first "capital" or "deadly" sin: pride. Now, insofar as pride is essentially about self-centeredness, mastery of the world, and making oneself the measure of all things, it should be apparent that cultivating the capabilities and attributes of fallen human beings might inadvertently foster pride. That is, although the goods and values of human nature are genuinely good and valuable, they are still wielded by the fallen hands of human beings, who might direct them to wrongful ends through their inherent proclivity to sin, the root of which is pride.

The quote also makes clear that this pride that affects "beings such as we are" can show itself in our grasping at self-centered mastery, and this is most severe when the cultivated goods and values of human nature usurp the place of faith, which must involve the opposite of pride: humility. Therefore, Newman states, culture can "impress us with a mere philosophical theory of life and conduct," something based in humanity itself, something within our own reach, our own goods and values, and therefore something that can make religion seem superfluous or even undesirable, thus usurping "the place of Revelation."[13]

Newman provides some more detail for his discussion of the dangers of pride and culture in a discussion of the beautiful, which serves as a counterpoint to the findings in our chapter on von Balthasar. As highlighted earlier, Newman argued that education should not be judged according to its usefulness, but as something "good in itself." Now, he amplifies his argument by arguing that to judge something according to its usefulness is to behold the true in terms of "power": "Useful Knowledge is the possession of truth as powerful."[14] This means that if human beings focus all their attention on what is useful, and what furthers their own ends, they limit the notion of the true to that which they can *use*, and the apprehension of truth thus becomes unavoidably self-centered. However, crucially, Newman also criticizes his own preferred attitude that education is "good in itself." He does not want to recant this position, but highlight its dangers, and how, if misappropriated, culture can become "an insidious and dangerous foe" of faith. He does this by arguing that to judge something as "good in itself" is, ultimately, to judge something as *beautiful*: cultivating our goods and values can lead to the "apprehension of [truth] as [the] beautiful."[15] Now, truth (as either power or beauty, but we will here concentrate on beauty), Newman claims, can and should make culture a "serviceable ally" of Christianity: "pursue it…to its furthest extent and its true limit, and you are led…to the Eternal and

Infinite, and the intimations of conscience and the announcement of the Church."[16] In other words, just as reason, as we noted, finds its home in God in that "a more penetrating knowledge will in turn call forth a greater faith," so should the beautiful perpetuate faith, bringing someone to the "Eternal and Infinite." However, insofar as the beautiful is apprehended *without* faith, in the fallen hands of prideful human beings, there is always a danger that it will become untethered from its home in God: "satisfy yourself with what is only visibly or intelligibly excellent, as you are likely to do [as fallen], and you will make...beauty the practical test of truth, and the sufficient object of the intellect."[17] A "sufficient object" is an object that suffices as end and goal, that fulfills the purposes of something. Culture, argues Newman, can then become an "insidious and dangerous foe" in becoming something sufficient in itself, in that the cultivation of the goods and values of human nature might lead one to decide one has no need of faith, or surreptitiously lead one to take mastery over one's own faith, by fostering the pride that makes one autonomous, which means "a law unto himself" (from the Greek word αὐτό [*auto*], meaning "self," and νομος [*nomos*], meaning "law"). Thus, we can extend Newman's comments about knowledge to culture, as something that "exerts a subtle influence in throwing us back on ourselves, and making us our own centre, and our minds the measure of all things,"[18] for the "perception of the Beautiful becomes the substitute for faith."

In "Discourse IX," Newman goes on to discuss the relationship between the Church and literature, and says the following about the way St. Philip Neri sought to evangelize culture: "Philip preferred, as he expressed it, tranquilly to cast his net to gain [souls]; he preferred to yield to the stream, and direct the current, which he could not stop, of science, literature, art & fashion, and to sweeten and to sanctify what God had made very good and man had spoilt." Initially, this sounds rather like Arrupe's "inculturation," which seeks to engage the terms of a "host" culture and "incarnate" Christ within it. But, there is a significant difference in Newman's interpretation of Neri; for he states that Neri's weapons were "unaffected humility and unpretending love."[19] That is, Newman feels that Neri does not just try to inculturate or incarnate Christ uncritically in a "host" culture, but concentrates on seeking to challenge the pride that very often attempts to cultivate the goods and values of human nature, with "unaffected humility." This evangelizing culture with a concern for "unaffected humility" takes shape elsewhere in Newman's thinking.

"SIMPLE ASSENT"

Focusing on our concern for evangelization, we will see that Newman's suspicion of culture presents a view of evangelizing as fostering what he terms "simple assent." Bearing in mind St. Philip Neri's comments about humility, we might ask what an emphasis on humility means for evangelizing culture. Most basically, evangelization would seem to be the bringing of an addressee to humility, the humility that is a sine qua non aspect of encountering God, sharply contradicting the self-orientation of pride. Examining this more closely, we turn to one of Newman's later works, *An Essay in Aid of a Grammar of Assent*. Here, Newman makes a distinction between what he calls two "habits of mind":[20] between apprehending "religious truth" and "theological truth." A proposition can be held as true, says Newman, in both "habits of mind"—and he gives an example with the statement that "there is One Personal and Present God." Held religiously, he says, this is a "reality," given in "devotion"; held theologically, it is apprehended for the purposes of "analysis and…[similar] intellectual exercises." These include "comparison, calculation, cataloguing, arranging, [and] classifying." Held religiously, what Newman calls "simple truth," a statement becomes a motive for "faithful obedience."[21] To assent to a proposition in the religious way of knowing is called by Newman "simple assent." It parallels directly the basic mode of human cognition we associate with sense experience. As he states, "There are many truths in concrete matter, which no one can demonstrate, yet everyone unconditionally accepts"—this is an "act of the intellect" described as "direct, absolute, complete in itself" and "unconditional."[22] To assent in the theological mode is a "complex assent"—an assent made "consciously and deliberately" and also connected with inferences, which are described as "both the antecedents of [complex] assent before assenting, and its usual concomitants after."[23]

What is interesting about Newman's work, here, is that he holds that "simple assent" in the "religious" habit of mind is *more important* than the "complex assent" of the theological mode. He gives an example with the proposition, "I believe what the Church proposes to be believed." He states that, as a real assent, this "is possible for the unlearned as well as the learned," *but* it "is imperative on learned as well as unlearned."[24] That is, our complex, inferential theological deliberations, are *having* to follow from "simple assent" to religious truth. This is because the "theological" habit of mind, if untethered and separated from the "religious," can lapse into pride, and, as with cultural sophistication, might even become an "insidious and dangerous foe," insofar as it can lead human beings to trust in their own resources, the goods and values of their intellect, rather than trusting in God.

For evangelization, we can now discern that the work of an evangelizer, in Newman's view, is to foster "simple assent," for this is the primary, central, fundamental, and unavoidable nexus of Catholic faith. This has certain consequences for how Newman would argue that we should understand the task of an evangelizer. First, in Newman's view, people are rarely converted by the strength of rational argument alone, for the virtue of humility is more far-reaching than something pertaining only to the abstract intellect. Second, and closely related to this, is the importance of an evangelizer being an obedient witness in his or her own life—for the "religious habit of mind" of "simple assent" is not about "notions" or "concepts," but about lived praxis, about people seeing for themselves what it is to participate in the sacramental life of Christ and his Church. Requiring further discussion is the third consequence—that seeking to foster "simple assent" calls for evangelizers to adopt a strategy of "reserve."

THE PRINCIPLE OF "RESERVE"

Newman adopts the radical position that culture can be a "foe" to faith even when it is essentially positive and edifying, when it cultivates the goods and values of human nature. Therefore, "simple assent"— saying yes to God in humility—can and must lie at the center of faith. Nonetheless, the theological traditions of the Church found in the *Catechism*, for example, demonstrate readily enough that much of it is very complex and, therefore, does not always seem likely to bring someone to a "real apprehension" of God, over against a "notional apprehension."

An evangelizer working in the spirit of Newman, then, should emphasize the simplicity of basic tenets of Catholic teaching: God as Creator of heaven and earth, the love of Jesus demonstrated on the cross of Calvary, the gift of the Holy Spirit imparted to the Church, and the sedimentation of the deposit of faith on these bases throughout the centuries. By doing so, other aspects of tradition will be reserved from proclamation, namely, the wealth of more complex and theological material, like the discussions surrounding God as Creator in relation to divine action, providence, and free will; or the precise understanding of the mechanics of the atonement wrought on Calvary; or the manifold ways in which the divinely connatural and hypostatic distinctness of the Son and Spirit were arrived at in Nicaea and Chalcedon. The point, here, is that, if "simple assent" is the nexus of faith, of bringing people to faith *in* God, rather than a conviction *that* God exists, we will need to *reserve* certain teachings, to ensure that faith *in* God is what we are proclaiming.

In numerous ways at different stages of his own journey in faith, Newman's theology has a theme of "reserve." It began in one of his earlier works, *The Arians of the Fourth Century*, which is a study of the Arian heresy and the triumph of orthodoxy through the theologians of the ancient Alexandrian Church. Here, he makes use of the idea that certain teachings of Church tradition were "set apart" or "reserved," and not revealed or proclaimed to those outside full communion with the Church: catechumens and pagans. These teachings were called by Church historians the *disciplina arcani*, or "secret/arcane discipline." He argues that the Alexandrian Church was known, particularly, for its "diligent and systematic preparation of candidates for baptism."[25] He claims that "before reception into…full discipleship," there was a two-to-three-year period of instruction in order that catechumens might "try their obedience" and be prepared for "revealed truth," that is, the "peculiar doctrines of the Gospel," or the secret "mysteries." Those who were unbaptized were taught only certain basic teachings, which we can consider would have cultivated what Newman would later call "simple assent." These teachings were "moral truths," namely, the necessity of obedience.[26] He refers here to the juxtaposition between "milk" and "solid food" of both the Letters to the Hebrews and 1 Corinthians, seeing so-called exoteric, or public teachings, as milk—and full-blown trinitarian dogma as "the strong meat of the Gospel." [27]

Newman's key sources include St. Cyril of Jerusalem, who is quoted as offering a tripartite division of Christian development—degrees on the way to full disclosure—working from simplicity to wisdom. At the highest level of the "elect," Newman sees the candidates being "entrusted with the knowledge of the Creed." Nonetheless, he states, even amongst the "elect," "the fully-developed doctrines" of the Trinity, incarnation, and atonement were "the exclusive possession of the serious and practiced Christian." [28] St. Clement, he says, also exhibits the "caution" that was "then adopted by Christians in teaching the truth": Clement saw the preliminary duty to those outside the flock as one of rousing the moral powers of the individual to "internal voluntary action," [29] that is, simple obedience to Jesus Christ.

In Newman's discussion in *Arians*, a key issue for him is the *protection* of those outside, or on the periphery of the flock—pagans and catechumens. He says that the Alexandrians "would write…with the *tenderness* or the reserve with which we…address those…whom we fear to mislead or prejudice against the truth." [30] He says that the use of such "caution" was the "result of the most truly charitable consideration for those…who were likely to be perplexed…by the sudden exhibition" of the "whole scheme." [31] Again, we read that to speak "indirectly" is a deliberate technique of St. Clement, intended to avoid causing injury to those who might not understand. [32] A key word of Newman's here is "duty." He says it was the "great duty of the Christian teacher…to unfold the sacred truths in due order," and that it is a matter of duty for the teacher "to present" the truth to his or her hearers, "with caution or reserve." [33]

This general sense of duty or responsibility for others can also be detected behind the concerns of the *Grammar*, and "simple assent" itself. He states in a discussion of trinitarian doctrine, that, if we focus on the "elaborate, subtle, [and] impregnable" formulation of a dogma, how can it "come to the afflicted," or, for that matter, "the unlearned, the young, the busy"? How can it be, he asks, "a fact which is to arrest them, penetrate them, and to support and animate them in their passage through life?" [34] It is again a matter of duty for Newman that we present Christian faith from the point where the "pulse of true theology beats," the point that invokes "loving obedience"—a point from which "security" can be imparted, but only as "the fruit of costly personal engagement, rather than its precondition."[35]

The theme of reserve in Newman's theology thus presents us with a further strategy of evangelization, by which we would "reserve" the more complex and theological elements of the Catholic teaching, so that our evangelizing work can "arrest" people, "penetrate" them, and then "support and animate them in their passage through life." Overall, we see with Newman that the work of evangelizing culture must always be on guard against seeming to offer people another "worldview" or "ideology," to compete with the manifold doctrines and perspectives on offer in the contemporary world. In the message of Christ and his Church, we are offering people something resonating with the deepest desires of their own hearts, which can only take hold of them if they say yes to God, and not through convincing them by adhering too closely to the terms of their own cultural setting, however impressive and sophisticated that setting might be.

MARY AS TOWER OF IVORY

Let us now bring this book to a close by gathering together the insights gained from this discussion of Newman through the last title of Mary to be discussed: Tower of Ivory. Mary as the Tower of Ivory, of course, resonates strongly with an approach to evangelization in the spirit of Newman, as ivory is an ancient symbol of purity and simplicity, with its shimmering whiteness being reminiscent of an addressee who has been purified or cleansed of the multicolored hues of his or her own cultural baggage, and brought to a point of simplicity—a point where only Christ can be seen, where Christ conquers all. Mary herself indeed exemplifies this posture of total and absolute Christ orientation, for, in Scripture, she never speaks of herself, except to say, "Here am I, the servant of the Lord; let it be with me according to your word" (Luke 1:38). But in this connection, Mary is also an exemplary figure for evangelizers themselves, for this pure-hearted Christ-centeredness is what Newman's work calls those who proclaim Jesus to seek. In this way, building on the prior exploration of Dorothy Day, we are reminded again that evangelizers must be perpetually evangelized, even converted, again and again, that anyone seeking to serve Christ and his Church must reach the point of "simple assent" prior to proclamation, and remain oriented by it *while* proclaiming; an evangelizer must always say, "Let it be with me according to your word."

The imagery of the Tower relates to Mary, as we have seen, in terms of signifying a reversal of worldly pride, power, and stability. This obviously connects also with our discussion of Newman, insofar as Newman's challenging questioning of even edifying culture radically upsets the way human beings seek to understand the world and flourish in it, through cultivating the goods and values of human nature. Nonetheless, in common parlance, "ivory towers" are a synonym for the precise opposite of what Newman is saying. This is, of course, a pejorative term usually applied to academia, as a realm of self-referential and seemingly meaningless inquiry, completely disconnected from real life and the "joys and hopes, griefs and sorrows" of humankind. Bearing this point in mind, we can see why this title is so important for evangelization, and even suggest that it should stand at the beating heart of evangelization. Indeed, one might even argue that the gleaming whiteness of this imagery could represent the light of Christ radiating outward from the heart of Mary as Star of Evangelization, the very nexus in relation to which the other approaches we have studied should be considered.

The reason for this centrality is, first, that although von Balthasar promised to hold together sowing the seed and tilling the soil, there was, with his approach, a danger of exclusivity based on cultural sophistication. Moreover, for very different reasons, there was a danger of exclusivity in the life and witness of Dorothy Day, on the basis that certain charisms of Christian life were greatly emphasized in her approach, arguably at the expense of other gifts. By focusing on "simple assent" and humility, by having our evangelizing work perpetually formed and reformed by pondering Mary as the Tower of Ivory, we are repeatedly reminded that the gospel of Jesus Christ is the antithesis of exclusivity. After all, an evangelizer is one called to proclaim and witness to all people in all times and places (cf. Mark 16:15; Matt 28:19). Jesus is the "light of all people" (John 1:4); God wants all people "to be saved and to come to knowledge of the truth" (1 Tim 2:4), and breaks down the barriers between peoples, with Christ himself as the embodiment of unity: there are no more distinctions, but "all of you are one in Christ Jesus" (Gal 3:28). Moreover, as we have seen, the universal breadth and range of the gospel message is explicitly directed to the most vulnerable—the poor—and these are often those for whom cultural sophistication is difficult or impossible to attain for practical reasons. But Newman reminds us that each of us is called to be poor by cultivating humility, or better, "poverty of spirit" (see Matt 5:3).

Jesus was sent "to bring good news to the poor" (Luke 4:18), and there are direct ramifications of this fact for his followers, who admonished against self-satisfaction, pride, or snobbishness of any kind, and the same mind must therefore "be in you that was in Christ Jesus" who "emptied himself, taking the form of a slave" (Phil 2:5, 7). So, Mary as Tower of Ivory is centrally important for this study as offering a wide-ranging, even a universal center of orientation for evangelization. Additionally, in Mary as Tower of Ivory, understood through the lens of Newman's "simple assent," we find that the two sides to Paul VI's central axis of evangelization, which has accompanied our inquiry throughout, are bound together tightly, without the restrictions we saw with the potential exclusivity of the *via pulchritudinis*. This suggests that we are at a juncture of considerable importance. If our witness and proclaiming of the gospel is simple, straightforward, and direct, Christ himself is the focus, which suggests that our evangelizing will be "understandable and persuasive." Of course, in being expressed simply, the teaching will be understandable. But by being cleansed of the accoutrements of cultural and intellectual sophistication, Christ himself can take hold of our work, and the Gospels make clear there is no more compelling figure than Jesus.

Importantly, moreover, evangelizing by fostering "simple assent," seeking after the moment whereby an addressee can surrender to Christ and say, "Let it be with me according to your word," is to maintain the "untouchable purity" of the message, for precisely the same reasons. That is, by focusing on the straightforward simplicity of the message and not engaging in any contrived attempts to manipulate or generate culturally directed responses, the "message of Christ in all its richness" can live in the hearts of those who hear it. This "living in the hearts" of human beings calls to mind the distinction made in the first chapter, between two distinct ways to approach the verb *to accommodate* in evangelization. First, it obviously means to inhabit or reside, to "live," and in relation to Paul

VI's untouchable purity, we are thus dealing with the message perduring authentically as itself in an addressee without adulteration. Second, however, it means to "fit" or "appropriate," in terms of rendering the message "suited" to different contexts and expectations. Mary as Tower of Ivory, exemplifying "simple assent," offers an accommodation with universal, central provenance, namely, humility or poverty of spirit. This is because Christ is the one who reveals to us what it is to be perfect in humanity, and Christ is the one who "humbled himself," suggesting that true human dignity, the heart of human life, is found in humility, found at the point where our limitedness is apprehended in the light of Christ, as *creatureliness*: a point where we are caught up in loving responsiveness to God's will alone.

In this binding together of both sides to Paul VI's central axis in a way which is genuinely universal, we have thus arrived at our destination, with the Tower of Ivory shining forth at the heart of Mary as the Star of Evangelization, so-called no doubt, in part, as one who radiates Christ's light in immaculate purity. That is, we find ourselves at the central juncture, namely, an understanding of tilling the soil and sowing the seed that lies at the very heart of life in Christ, a life overflowing into the lives of others, whom God wants to be saved and to come to knowledge of the truth (1 Tim 2:4).

Notes

INTRODUCTION

1. For examples, cf. Matt 28:18; Mark 16:15; 1 Cor 9:16; *Gaudium et Spes* 3 (the Church "seeks but a solitary goal: to carry forward the work of Christ" in bearing "witness to the truth"); *Lumen Gentium* 17; *Redemptoris Missio* 1.

2. Key papal documents following *Evangelii Nuntiandi* by John Paul II include primarily *Redemptoris Misso* (1990), and also *Catechesi Tradendae* (1979), *Chris-tifideles Laici* (1988), *Tertio Millennio Adveniente* (1994), *Ecclesia in America* (1999), and *Novo Millennio Ineunte* (2001). For Benedict XVI, see *Ubicumque et Semper* (2010) and *Porta Fidei* (2011). For Pope Francis, see particularly *Evangelii Gaudium* (2014).

3. For a summary of the *content* of evangelization, see *Evangelii Nuntiandi* 15: "The promises of the New Alliance in Jesus Christ, the teaching of the Lord and the apostles, the Word of life, the sources of grace and of God's loving kindness, the path of salvation."

4. *Dei Filius* 3 (au. emphasis); cf. also *Dei Verbum* 5.

5. Clifford Geertz, *The Interpretation of Cultures* (New York: Basic Books, 1973), 5.

6. Joseph Ratzinger, *Daughter Zion* (San Francisco: Ignatius Press, 1983), 12.

7. Cf. particularly Prov 8 and Wis 7.

8. Ratzinger, *Daughter Zion*, 26–27.

9. See, for example, *Tertio Millenio Adveniente* (§59) and *Novo Millenio Ineunte* (§58).

10. Joseph Ratzinger, "My Word shall not return to me empty!" in Ratzinger and Hans Urs von Balthasar, *Mary: The Church at Source* (San Francisco: Ignatius Press, 2005), 16.

11. *Catechism of the Catholic Church* 1822.

12. Ratzinger and von Balthasar, *Mary: The Church at Source*, 17.

13. F. L. Cross and E. A. Livingstone, eds., *Oxford Dictionary of the Christian Church* (Oxford: Oxford University Press, 2005), 920.

14. Quoted by T. J. Gorringe, *Furthering Humanity: A Theology of Culture* (Aldershot, UK: Ashgate, 2004), 4.

15. G. Hartman, *The Fateful Question of Culture* (New York: Columbia University Press, 1997), 172.

16. See Luigi Gambero, *Mary and the Fathers of the Church: The Blessed Virgin Mary in Patristic Thought* (San Francisco: Ignatius Press, 1999), 57; Tina Beattie, "Mary in Patristic Theology," in *Mary: The Complete Resource*, ed. Sarah Jane Boss (Oxford: Oxford University Press, 2007), 75–105, at 77.

17. Gregory of Nyssa, "De caeco et Zachaeo 4," in Migne, *Patrologia Graeca* 59, 605; Origen, *Homilies on Exodus* 10.4, *Patrologia Graeca*, 12, 374.

18. Ambrose, *De Virginitate* 4, 20, in Migne, *Patrologia Latina* 16, 271.

19. Joseph Cardinal Ratzinger (Pope Benedict XVI), "My Word shall not return to me empty!" Sermon delivered at the German Bishops' Conference in Stapelfeld, Germany (March 6, 1979), 14.

20. Louis de Montfort, *True Devotion to Mary* (North Carolina: Tan Books, 2010), 137 and 164; "strike the roots" on pages 14–15, but this subclause from the Vulgate is not found in modern translations of Ecclesiasticus (Sirach).

21. Although linked to the Holy House of Loreto, this litany is thought to originate much earlier in the Dominican tradition; see *The Oxford Dictionary of the Christian Church*, 990–91.

22. See also John Paul II, "Address at the Opening of the Fourth General Conference of Latin American Bishops" (October 12, 1992), 24: *AAS* 85 (1993), 826.

23. Cf. Thomas Aquinas *S.Th.*, II-II, q.2, a.2.

24. Aquinas, *S.Th.*, II-II, q.2, a.2.

25. Aquinas, *S.Th.*, I, q.93. ad. 4.

26. Isa 61:10, quoted from *Evangelii Gaudium* 116; cf. John Paul II, *Ecclesia in Africa* 61.

CHAPTER 1. THE THEOLOGICAL COORDINATES OF CULTURE IN *GAUDIUM ET SPES*

1. All quotes from *Gaudium et Spes* in this work are taken from Paul VI, *Gaudium et Spes*, December 7, 1965, papal archive, the Holy See, http://www.vatican.va/archive/hist_councils/ii_vatican_council/documents/vat-ii_const_19651207_gaudium-et-spes_en.html.

Notes

2. This is seen, for example, in important developments like promulgating the Dogma of the Immaculate Conception (1854), and the concerns of the First Vatican Council, which, while including currents of thought arising from the Enlightenment (e.g., rationalism) did not systematically engage with their *cultural* manifestations. The term *drama* for Modernism taken from Joseph Ratzinger, *Milestones: Memoirs 1927–1977* (San Francisco: Ignatius Press, 1997), 108.

3. Brian Davies, *The Thought of Thomas Aquinas* (Oxford: Clarendon Press, 1992), 241.

4. That said, this flagship conciliar concern is not found in Aquinas himself, obviously, for he is a premodern figure.

5. Davies, *Aquinas*, 241.

6. Edmund Burke, *Reflections on the Revolution in France* (London: J. Dodsley, 1789), 84.

7. T. S. Eliot, *Notes towards a Definition of Culture* (London: Faber & Faber, 1962), 14.

8. For a full discussion of the issues surrounding atheism and Vatican II, see Stephen Bullivant, *The Salvation of Atheists and Catholic Dogmatic Theology* (Oxford: Oxford University Press, 2010).

9. These two tendencies are often linked with the Thomist affirmation of the good of human nature on the optimistic side, and the Augustinian emphasis on the severity of the fall, on the negative side.

10. Herbert Vorgrimler, *Commentary on the Documents of Vatican II*, vol. 5 (London: Burns & Oates, 1969), 69–70.

11. Charles Moeller, "History of the Constitution" [*Gaudium et Spes*] in Vorgrimler, *Commentary*, 1–76, at 22.

12. Moeller, "History of the Constitution," 29.

13. Moeller, "History of the Constitution," 29 (translation altered).

14. Moeller, "History of the Constitution," 52.

15. Moreller, "History of the Constitution," 60.

16. Austin Flannery, *Vatican Council II: The Conciliar and Postconciliar Documents*, (Collegeville, MN: Liturgical Press, 1996), 959, §55.

17. Roberto Tucci, "The Proper Development of Culture," in Vorgrimler, *Commentary*, 246–87, at 260.

18. Tucci, "The Proper Development of Culture," 260.

19. Tucci, "The Proper Development of Culture," 264.

20. Dondeyne quoted by Tucci, "The Proper Development of Culture," 262.

21. Moeller, "History of the Constitution," 61.

22. Flannery, *Vatican Council II*, 963, §59.

CHAPTER 2. INCULTURATION: MARY AS "MIRROR OF JUSTICE"

1. Flannery, *Vatican Council II*, 963n7, §59.
2. Author's emphasis.
3. See Kevin Burke's introduction to *Pedro Arrupe: Essential Writings*, ed. Kevin F. Burke (Maryknoll, NY: Orbis Books, 2004), for a good discussion of Arrupe's life.
4. Pedro Arrupe, *Jesuit Apostolates Today: An Anthology of Letters and Addresses III*, ed. Jerome Aixala (Anand, India: Sahitya Prakash, 1981), 171.
5. Peter Schineller, *A Handbook on Inculturation* (New York: Paulist Press, 1990), 22.
6. Arrupe, *Jesuit Apostolates Today*, 173.
7. Arrupe, *Jesuit Apostolates Today*, 171.
8. Arrupe, *Jesuit Apostolates Today*, 176.
9. Ignatius Loyola, *The Spiritual Exercises*, trans. Michael Ivens (Leominster: Gracewing, 2012), 33.
10. Ignatius, *The Spiritual Exercises*, 34.
11. Ignatius, *The Spiritual Exercises*, 34.
12. Joseph Ratzinger, *Daughter Zion* (San Francisco: Ignatius Press, 1983), 17.
13. Susan Sontag, "The Anthropologist as Hero," in *Against Interpretation and Other Essays* (London: Penguin Classics, 2009), 69–81, at 69.
14. Sontag, "Anthropologist," 72.
15. Arrupe, *Jesuit Apostolates Today*, 179.
16. Schineller, *Inculturation*, 22.
17. Sontag, "Anthropologist," 69–70, 74.
18. Arrupe, *Jesuit Apostolates Today*, 173.
19. Arrupe, *Jesuit Apostolates Today*, 174.
20. Arrupe, *Jesuit Apostolates Today*, 174 (au. emphasis).
21. Ignatius, *Spiritual Exercises*, 34.
22. Arrupe, *Essential Writings*, 151, 159, 172.
23. Josef Pieper, *The Four Cardinal Virtues* (South Bend, IN: University of Notre Dame Press, 1966), 44.
24. Quoted by Pieper, *Virtues*, 44n9.
25. K. I. Onesti and M. T. Brauch, "Righteousness, Righteousness of God," in *Dictionary of Paul and His Letters: A Compendium of Contemporary Biblical Scholarship*, ed. Gerald Hawthorne, Ralph P. Martin, and Daniel G. Reid (Downers Grove, IL: InterVarsity Press, 1993), 827–37.

26. Onesti and Brauch, "Righteousness," 827–37.

27. Arrupe, *Jesuit Apostolates Today*, 177.

28. Author's emphasis.

29. For an excellent critical edition of the Protoevangelium of James, see Emile de Strycker, *La Forme la plus ancienne du Protévangile de Jacques*, Subsidia Hagiographica 33 (Brussels: Société des Bollandistes, 1961), or an English translation in James Keith Elliot, *The Apocryphal New Testament* (Oxford: Clarendon Press, 1993).

CHAPTER 3. INCULTURALITY: MARY AS "SEAT OF WISDOM"

1. Indeed, truth is arguably the most pervasive theme in Ratzinger's writings, seen in his discussion of the scholastic *verum est ens* (being is truth) in Joseph Ratzinger, *Introduction to Christianity* (London: Burns & Oates, 1969), 34, and even in his discussion of his episcopal motto "co-worker in truth" in his final autobiographical work, Benedict XVI and Peter Seewald, *Last Testament: Benedict XVI in His Own Words*, trans. Jacob Phillips (London: Bloomsbury, 2016), 241.

2. See Catholic News Agency, "Pople Tells Why He Chose the Name of Benedict XVI," accessed March 27, 2018, http://www.catholicnewsagency.com/resources/benedict-xvi/life-and-ministry/pope-tells-why-he-chose-the-name-of-benedict-xvi/.

3. See UCA News, "Cardinal Ratzinger Urges Asian Bishops to Adopt Term 'Inter-culturality,'" March 9, 1993, http://www.ucanews.com/story-archive/?post_name=/1993/03/09/cardinal-ratzinger-urges-asian-bishops-to-adopt-term-interculturality&post_id=42924.

4. Joseph Ratzinger, "Christ, Faith and the Challenge of Cultures," 1, accessed March 27, 2018, http://www.ewtn.com/library/CURIA/RATZHONG.HTM.

5. Ratzinger, "Christ, Faith and the Challenge," 1A.

6. Ratzinger, "Christ, Faith and the Challenge," 1.

7. Ratzinger, "Christ, Faith and the Challenge," 1C.

8. Ratzinger, "Christ, Faith and the Challenge," 1C.

9. Ratzinger, "Christ, Faith and the Challenge," 1C (au. emphasis).

10. Benedict XVI states that "we cannot say 'I have the truth,' but the truth has us, it touches us" and so we should "try to let ourselves be guided by this touch." Benedict XVI and Seewald, *Last Testament*, 41.

11. Joseph Ratzinger, "Culture and Truth: Some Reflections on the Encyclical Letter, *Fides et Ratio*," given on Saturday, February 13, 1999, in the

Chapel at St. Patrick's Seminary. Lecture, *Patrician Magazine*, February 1999; http://www.mtsm.org/pdf/cardratzingeronfidesetratio.pdf.

12. Ratzinger, "Culture and Truth."

13. Ratzinger, "Culture and Truth."

14. Ratzinger, "Christ, Faith and the Challenge," 2.

15. Ratzinger, "Christ, Faith and the Challenge."

16. Ratzinger, "Christ, Faith and the Challenge," 1C. Note wording altered slightly as original erroneously has "formally" in place of "formerly."

17. Ratzinger, "Christ, Faith and the Challenge," 1C.

18. Edmund Burke, *Reflections on the Revolution in France* (London: J. Dodsley, 1789), 84.

19. Brian Davies, *The Thought of Thomas Aquinas* (Oxford: Clarendon Press, 1992), 241.

20. Sarah Jane Boss, "The Virgin's Cult," in *Mary: The Complete Resource*, ed. Sarah Jane Boss (Oxford: Oxford University Press, 2007), 161.

21. Boss, "The Virgin's Cult," 168.

22. Boss, "The Virgin's Cult," 161–70.

CHAPTER 4. BEAUTY: MARY AS "MYSTICAL ROSE"

1. Hans Urs von Balthasar, *The Glory of the Lord*, vol. 1, *Seeing the Form* (San Francisco: Ignatius Press, 1982), 10.

2. Hans Urs von Balthasar, *Theo-Logic* (San Francisco: Ignatius Press, 2004); Hans Urs von Balthasar, *Theo-Drama* (San Francisco: Ignatius Press, 1988).

3. Benedict XVI and Peter Seewald, *Last Testament*, trans. Jacob Phillips (London: Bloomsbury, 2016).

4. Hans Urs von Balthasar, *Apokalypse der deutschen Seele: Studien zu einer Lehre von letzten Haltungen* (Freiburg: Johannes Verlag, 1998).

5. Marc Ouellet, "Hans Urs von Balthasar: Witness to the Integration of Faith and Culture," *Communio* (Spring 1991): 111–26, at 114.

6. Henri de Lubac, "A Witness of Christ in the Church: Hans Urs von Balthasar," eulogy at Balthasar's funeral, available at https://www.crossroadsinitiative.com/library_article/757/Hans_Urs_von_Balthasar_Eulogy_de_Lubac.html (accessed March 27, 2018).

7. Joseph Ratzinger, "Homily at the Funeral Liturgy for Hans Urs von Balthasar," *Communio* 15, no. 4 (Winter 1988): 512–16.

8. For example, in Ratzinger, *Daughter Zion: Meditations on the Church's Marian Belief* (San Francisco: Ignatius Press, 1983), 8.

9. von Balthasar, *The Glory of the Lord*, 22.

10. von Balthasar, *The Glory of the Lord*, 9.

11. John Henry Newman, *An Essay in Aid of a Grammar of Assent* (South Bend, IN: Notre Dame Press, 1979), 122.

12. von Balthasar, *The Glory of the Lord*, 17

13. von Balthasar, *The Glory of the Lord*, 17 (au. emphasis).

14. von Balthasar, *The Glory of the Lord*, 9.

15. von Balthasar, *The Glory of the Lord*, 18.

16. von Balthasar, *The Glory of the Lord*, 19.

17. von Balthasar, *The Glory of the Lord*, 38.

18. von Balthasar, *The Glory of the Lord*, 20.

19. Ouellet, "Witness to the Integration," 123.

20. John Henry Newman, *An Essay in Aid of a Grammar of Assent*, ed. Ian Ker (Oxford: Clarendon Press, 1985), 9.

21. Hans Urs von Balthasar, *Love Alone* (New York: Herder & Herder, 1969), 47.

22. von Balthasar, *Love Alone*, 49.

23. von Balthasar, *The Glory of the Lord*, 30–31, 33.

24. von Balthasar, *The Glory of the Lord*, 37.

25. Ouellet, "Witness to the Integration," 117–18.

26. Ouellet, "Witness to the Integration," 122 (au. emphasis).

27. von Balthasar, *The Glory of the Lord*, 18.

28. von Balthasar, *Love Alone*, 45.

29. von Balthasar, *The Glory of the Lord*, 20.

30. Although, the original Hebrew almost certainly does not mean "rose" as we understand it today, but something closer to "tulip."

31. Matthias Scheeben, quoted in von Balthasar, *The Glory of the Lord*, 110–11.

32. von Balthasar, *The Glory of the Lord*, 28.

33. Cf. Father Zossima in Fyodor Dostoyevsky, *The Brothers Karamazov*, trans. Constance Garnett (Mineola, NY: Dover Publications, 2005), 48.

CHAPTER 5. WITNESS: MARY AS "TOWER OF DAVID"

1. See the short biography in Jacob Phillips, "'Being Scorned by One's Own Is Perfect Joy': The Strange Case of Dorothy Day," *Journal of Religious History* 37, no. 4 (2013): 528–40.

2. See Phillips, "Being Scorned by One's Own."

3. Quoted in Robert Ellsberg, "Introduction," Dorothy Day, *The Duty of Delight* (Milwaukee: Marquette University Press, 2011), xiii–xxvi.

4. See Ashley Beck, "Making the Encyclicals Click," *New Blackfriars* 93, no. 1044 (March 2012): 213–29.

5. See examples in Phillips, "Being Scorned by One's Own," 527.

6. Day, *The Duty of Delight*, 449.

7. Figures from Ashley Beck, *Dorothy Day* (London: Catholic Truth Society, 2008), 34.

8. Beck, *Dorothy Day*, 1.

9. Beck, *Dorothy Day*, 3.

10. Beck, *Dorothy Day*, 3.

11. Beck, *Dorothy Day*, 4.

12. Aidan Nichols, *The Shape of Catholic Theology* (Collegeville, MN: Liturgical Press, 1991), 36.

13. Day, *The Duty of Delight*, 30.

14. Brigid O'Shea Merriman, *Searching for Christ: The Spirituality of Dorothy Day* (South Bend, IN: University of Notre Dame Press, 2001), 34, cf. n25.

15. As listed in the *Compendium of the Catechism of the Catholic Church*, there are also seven complementary "Spiritual Works of Mercy," which Day was certainly aware of, although the corporal works were always the emphasis of the Catholic Worker.

16. Dorothy Day's engaging with active political resistance should be mentioned as an aspect of her life and witness that interested readers are recommended to explore further.

17. Quoted in O'Shea Merriman, *Spirituality*, from *The Catholic Worker* newspaper, May 1939.

18. Quoted in O'Shea Merriman, *Spirituality*, 55, from *The Catholic Worker* newspaper, May 1936.

19. Quoted in O'Shea Merriman, *Spirituality*, 160. See also Dorothy Day, *The Long Loneliness* (New York: Harper & Brothers, 1952), 181, where Day speaks of being involved in a "class war, using such weapons as the works of mercy for the immediate means to show our love and alleviate suffering."

20. Beck, *Dorothy Day*, 1 (au. emphasis).

21. Day, *The Duty of Delight*, 63.

22. Day, *The Duty of Delight*, 73.

23. Day, *The Long Loneliness*, 257–58.

24. St. Thérèse of Lisieux, *The Story of a Soul*, ed. Mother Agnes of Jesus, trans. Michael Day, Cong. Orat. (Charlotte, NC: Tan Books, 2010), 42–43.

25. St. Thérèse of Lisieux, *The Story of a Soul*, 43.

26. St. Thérèse of Lisieux, *The Story of a Soul*, 88 and 115.
27. Day, *The Duty of Delight*, 73.
28. Day, *The Long Loneliness*.
29. Day, *The Duty of Delight*, 228 and 230.
30. Dietrich Bonhoeffer, *Dietrich Bonhoeffer Works in English*, vol. 4, *Discipleship*, German edition ed. Martin Kuske and Ilse Tödt; English edition ed. Geffrey B. Kelly and John D. Godsey; trans. Barbara Green and Reinhard Krauss (Minneapolis: Fortress, 2003), 154.
31. Avery Dulles, "The Threefold Office of the Church in Newman's Ecclesiology," in *Newman after a Hundred Years*, ed. Ian Ker and A. G. Hill (Oxford: Clarendon Press, 1990), 375–99, at 379.
32. Dulles, "Threefold Office," 380.

CHAPTER 6. SIMPLE ASSENT: MARY AS "TOWER OF IVORY"

1. George Abbot-Smith, *A Manual Lexicon of the Greek New Testament* (London: T&T Clark, 1999), 48.
2. Quoted in Emery de Gaál, *The Theology of Pope Benedict XVI: The Christocentric Shift* (New York: Palgrave Macmillan 2010), 55.
3. Ian Ker and Terrence Mulligan, "Introduction," in *Cambridge Companion to John Henry Newman*, ed. Ian Ker and Terence Mulligan (Cambridge: Cambridge University Press, 2009), xi.
4. Ian Ker, *Newman: The Fullness of Christianity* (London: Bloomsbury, 2009), 1.
5. John Coulson, *The Rediscovery of Newman: An Oxford Symposium* (London: Sheed & Ward, 1967), xx.
6. Ker, *Newman*, 1.
7. Ker, *Newman*, 1.
8. Meriol Treviol, *The Pillar of Cloud* (London: Macmillan & Co, 1962), 442.
9. John Henry Newman, *The Idea of a University* (New Haven, CT: Yale University Press 1996), 148.
10. Newman, *The Idea of a University*, 77.
11. Newman, *The Idea of a University*, 148–49.
12. Newman, *The Idea of a University*, 150.
13. Newman, *The Idea of a University*, 150.
14. Newman, *The Idea of a University*, 150.
15. Newman, *The Idea of a University*, 150.

16. Newman, *The Idea of a University*, 150.

17. Newman, *The Idea of a University*, 151.

18. Newman, *The Idea of a University*, 151.

19. Newman, *The Idea of a University*, 162.

20. Nicholas Lash, introduction to *An Essay in Aid of a Grammar of Assent* (South Bend, IN: Notre Dame Press, 1979), 15n69.

21. Newman, *Grammar*, 108, 115, 122.

22. Newman, *Grammar*, 135, 157.

23. Newman, *Grammar*, 157.

24. Newman, *Grammar*, 131.

25. John Henry Newman, *The Arians of the Fourth Century* (South Bend, IN: Notre Dame Press, 2001), 41.

26. Newman, *Arians*, 45.

27. Newman, *Arians*, 45.

28. Newman, *Arians*, 45.

29. Newman, *Arians*, 48–49.

30. Newman, *Arians*, 42 (au. emphasis).

31. Newman, *Arians*, 45–46.

32. Newman, *Arians*, 45.

33. Newman, *Arians*, 48, 72.

34. Newman, *Grammar*, 112–13.

35. Nicholas Lash, "Introduction," in Newman, *Grammar*, 19.

Bibliography

MAGISTERIAL DOCUMENTS

Catechesi Tradendae
Christifideles Laici
Dei Filius
Dei Verbum
Ecclesia in Africa
Ecclesia in America
Evangelii Gaudium
Evangelii Nuntiandi
Gaudium et Spes
Lumen Gentium
Novo Millennio Ineunte
Porta Fidei
Redemptoris Missio
Tertio Millennio Adveniente
Ubicumque et Semper

BOOKS AND ARTICLES

Arrupe, Pedro. *Essential Writings*. Edited by Kevin Burke. Maryknoll, NY: Orbis Books, 2004.

————. *Jesuit Apostolates Today: An Anthology of Letters and Addresses III*. Edited by Jerome Aixala. Anand, India: Sahitya Prakash, 1981.

Balthasar, Hans Urs von. *Apokalypse der deutschen Seele: Studien zu einer Lehre von letzten Haltungen*. Freiburg: Johannes Verlag, 1998.

————. *The Glory of the Lord*. Vol. 1, *Seeing the Form*. San Francisco: Ignatius Press, 1982.

————. *Love Alone*. New York: Herder & Herder, 1969.

————. *Theo-Drama*. San Francisco: Ignatius Press, 1988.

————. *Theo-Logic*. San Francisco: Ignatius Press, 2004.

Beck, Ashley. *Dorothy Day*. London: Catholic Truth Society, 2008.

————. "Making the Encyclicals Click." *New Blackfriars* 93, no. 1044 (March 2012): 213–29.

Benedict XVI and Peter Seewald. *Last Testament*. Translated by Jacob Phillips. London: Bloomsbury, 2016.

Bonhoeffer, Dietrich. *Dietrich Bonhoeffer Works in English*. Volume 4, *Discipleship*. Translated by Barbara Green and Reinhard Krauss. Minneapolis: Fortress, 2003.

Boss, Sarah Jane, ed. *Mary: The Complete Resource*. Oxford, Oxford University Press, 2007.

Bullivant, Stephen. *The Salvation of Atheists and Catholic Dogmatic Theology*. Oxford: Oxford University Press, 2010.

Burke, Edmund. *Reflections on the Revolution in France*. London: J. Dodsley, 1789.

Cross, F. L., and E. A. Livingstone, eds. *Oxford Dictionary of the Christian Church*. Oxford: Oxford University Press 2005.

Davies, Brian. *The Thought of Thomas Aquinas*. Oxford: Clarendon Press, 1992.

Day, Dorothy. *The Duty of Delight*. Milwaukee: Marquette University Press, 2011.

————. *The Long Loneliness*. New York: Harper & Brothers, 1952.

Elliot, James. *The Apocryphal New Testament*. Oxford: Clarendon Press, 1993.

Eliot, T. S. *Notes toward a Definition of Culture*. London: Faber & Faber, 1962.

Gambero, Luigi. *Mary and the Fathers of the Church: The Blessed Virgin Mary in Patristic Thought*. San Francisco: Ignatius Press, 1999.

Geertz, Clifford. *The Interpretation of Cultures*. New York: Basic Books 1973.

Gorringe, T. J. *Furthering Humanity: A Theology of Culture*. Aldershot, UK: Ashgate, 2004.

Hartman, G. *The Fateful Question of Culture*. New York: Columbia University Press, 1997.

Ker, Ian, and A. G. Hill, eds. *Newman after a Hundred Years*. Oxford: Clarendon Press, 1990.

Lisieux, St Thérèse. *The Story of a Soul*. Edited by Mother Agnes of Jesus. Translated by Michael Day, Cong. Orat. Charlotte, NC: Tan Books, 2010.

Loyola, St. Ignatius. *The Spiritual Exercises*. Translated by Michael Ivens. Leominster: Gracewing, 2012.

Merriman, Brigid O'Shea. *Searching for Christ: The Spirituality of Dorothy Day*. South Bend, IN: University of Notre Dame Press, 2001.

Montfort, Louis de. *True Devotion to Mary*. Charlotte, NC: Tan Books, 2010.

Newman, John Henry. *An Essay in Aid of a Grammar of Assent*. South Bend, IN: University of Notre Dame Press, 1979.

Nichols, Aidan. *The Shape of Catholic Theology*. Collegeville, MN: Liturgical Press, 1991.

Onesti, K. I., and M. T. Brauch. "Righteousness, Righteousness of God." In *Dictionary of Paul and His Letters: A Compendium of Contemporary Biblical Scholarship*, edited by Gerald Hawthorne, Ralph P. Martin, and Daniel G. Reid. Downers Grove, IL: InterVarsity Press, 1993.

Ouellet, Marc. "Hans Urs von Balthasar: Witness to the Integration of Faith and Culture." *Communio* (Spring 1991): 111–26.

Phillips, Jacob. "'Being Scorned by One's Own Is Perfect Joy': The Strange Case of Dorothy Day." *Journal of Religious History*, 37 no. 4 (2013): 528–40.

Pieper, Josef. *The Four Cardinal Virtues*. South Bend, IN: University of Notre Dame Press, 1966.

Ratzinger, Joseph. "Culture and Truth: Some Reflections on the Encyclical Letter, *Fides et Ratio*." Presentation given on Saturday, February 13, 1999, in the Chapel at St. Patrick's Seminary. *The Patrician* (Winter 1999).

———. *Daughter Zion*. San Francisco: Ignatius Press, 1983.

———. *Introduction to Christianity*. London: Burns & Oates, 1969.

———. *Milestones: Memoirs 1927–1977*. San Francisco: Ignatius Press, 1997.

Ratzinger, Joseph, and Hans Urs von Balthasar. *Mary: The Church at the Source*. San Francisco: Ignatius Press, 2005.

Schineller, Peter. *A Handbook on Inculturation*. New York: Paulist Press, 1990.

Sontag, Susan. *Against Interpretation and Other Essays*. London: Penguin Classics, 2009.

Strycker, Emile de. *La Forme la plus ancienne du Protévangile de Jacques*. Subsidia Hagiographica, 33. Brussels: Société des Bollandistes, 1961.

Vorgrimler, Herbert. *Commentary on the Documents of Vatican II*. Vol. 5. London: Burns & Oates, 1969.

Index

Index

Thomas Aquinas, 14, 15, 25, 27, 53, 72, 102

Truth, 68–70, 83–86

Universal Declaration of Human Rights, 52–53

Veritatis Splendor (John Paul II), 83–85

von Balthasar, Hans Urs, 16, 77–83, 86–95, 128

Wisdom, 4, 71–74